A NATURALISTIC INTRODUCTION TO PHILOSOPHY

An Understanding of the Discipline of Naturalistic Studies and its Relationship with Philosophy, Naturalism, and Science

Second Edition

Amir Salehi, Ph.D.

Maple Creek Media
Hampstead ◊ Maryland ◊ United States

Printed in the United States of America

ISBN-13: 9781942914211
ISBN-10: 1942914210

MAPLE CREEK MEDIA

P.O. Box 624
Hampstead, MD 21074
Toll-Free Phone: 1-877-866-8820
Toll-Free Fax: 1-877-778-3756
Email: info@maplecreekmedia.com
Website: www.maplecreekmedia.com

Introduction

This second edition of "A Naturalistic Introduction to Philosophy" contains additional chapters and improvements to introducing philosophy naturalistically, as it was originally intended. The first five introductory chapters Metaphilosophy, Critical Thinking/Logic, Ethics, Metaphysics and Epistemology are virtually unchanged and like the first edition, they are best suited for students taking my classes physically. Due to the emphasis on methodology in this edition, some explanations remain short. I recommend that students become familiar with additional materials, in print and online, to gain a complete understanding of the history of and problems associated with the contents of the text.

It is impossible to understand Naturalistic perspectives without first having some understanding of the classic (Greek) approach. This is why the first five chapters provide the traditional views, which can be used as stepping stones towards the naturalistic perspectives and interpretations that are offered in later chapters. This arrangement clearly illustrates the similarities and differences among the naturalistic and traditional philosophical views.

Unlike the first edition, this second edition would suffice as a supplementary source for instructors teaching upper division or advanced courses in Epistemology, Metaphysics, Analytic Philosophy, Philosophy of Science and the subject for which it is intended, Naturalism. In this regard, I recommend instructors use chapters 6, 7 and 10 for upper division courses, chapters 8 and 9 for advanced courses.

Contents

Chapter 1
Metaphilosophy (What is Philosophy?)

This chapter has two objectives:

A)   Explain what is meant by Metaphilosophy and

B)   Clarify the issue of "progress" in Philosophy

Philosophy is defined historically as Love of Wisdom (*Philo + Sophia*), but this definition cannot say much about what a philosophical activity is, including what should be the approach for answering philosophical questions.

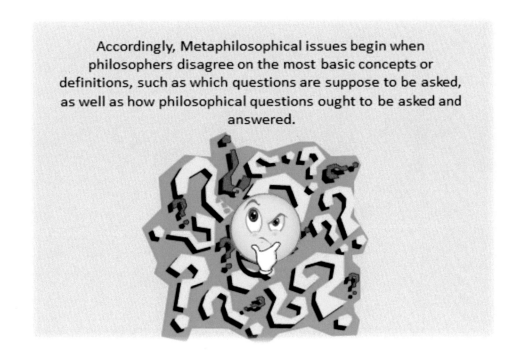

Accordingly, Metaphilosophical issues begin when philosophers disagree on the most basic concepts or definitions, such as which questions are suppose to be asked, as well as how philosophical questions ought to be asked and answered.

Generally speaking, all the questions related to the nature of philosophy, such as the subject, method, and purpose, are considered as Metaphilosophical questions. Metaphilosophy is therefore a branch of philosophy, or a philosophical discipline, that is concerned with philosophy itself. Metaphilosophy is also known as Philosophy of Philosophy (META is derived from the Greek language and is a prefix used in English in order to indicate a concept that is an abstraction from another concept, used to complete or add to the latter).

Further, Metaphilosophical issues include what constitutes "truth," what is the preferred method for establishing knowledge claims, etc.

Is this true or not? How do I know if this is true?

Similarly, all chemists around the world have a universal language and method as far as how to perform experiments and how to evaluate data. In addition, the lack of a universal method for establishing truth makes it difficult to have what the sciences often proudly refer to, namely "progress."

Specifically, while it appears that philosophers are stuck in a never-ending debate over the most basic concepts and definitions, the sciences, especially the natural sciences, can point to their technological achievements and claim progress in their respected theoretical activities.

What we can learn here is the relationship that Philosophy has to its history is not the same as the relationship sciences have to their history.

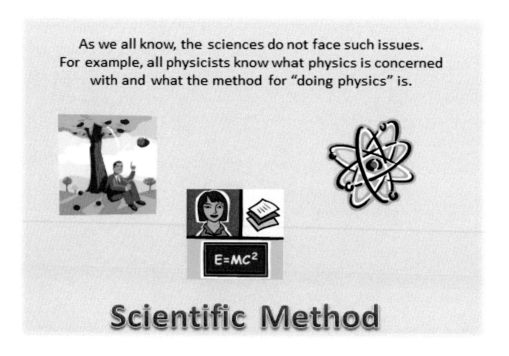

As we all know, the sciences do not face such issues. For example, all physicists know what physics is concerned with and what the method for "doing physics" is.

E=MC²

Scientific Method

We know for example that merely by studying the history of physics, one cannot be called scientist, since the history of science in general is about who has discovered what, when, and perhaps how, while "doing Physics" means that one actually applies the knowledge.

In the above classifications, although contemporary philosophy may be understood as a response to Modernism, and Modernism as a response to Medieval Philosophy, it would be a misunderstanding to interpret these changes as "historical progress," because each of the above historical contexts was shaped by certain social and cultural interests, and therefore it is difficult to claim "progress."

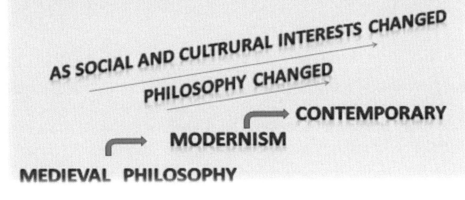

The classic picture of "doing science" is that the scientist constructs an experiment in a lab, collects data, makes predictions, draws conclusions, etc. Unfortunately, the same relationship cannot be claimed in philosophy, because philosophical issues seem to be embedded in their historical context and consequently, one cannot study philosophy without studying its history and associated social/cultural framework.

Scientific Method:

See a problem
Collect Data
Form an Hypothesis
Perform an Experiment
Draw Conclusion
Check Conclusion

All things considered, the Metaphilosophical question that presents itself at this point is: Is there any philosophical view that can transcend its historical context? Or is there a philosophical view that is trans-cultural?

Participate in the following discussion by answering the question below:

1) Is there or can there ever be "progress" in Philosophy?

Help: If you are answering this question with YES, then you are stating that Philosophy has its own agendas and that the "objective" is to <u>come forward</u> by answering specific questions "correctly."

If you are answering the above question with NO, then you are stating that philosophical debates by their very nature MUST presuppose fundamental disagreements about issues because they look at problems from different views <u>without pursuing a final/"correct" answer</u>. Explain your answer in 2 to 3 paragraphs.

SUBJECT OF PHILOSOPHY

The question "What is the subject of Philosophy" is what philosophers are concerned with, or what they are interested in.

For example, psychologists are interested in "examining" human behavior, and astronomers are interested in studying stars, planets, nebulas, and galaxies. So what is the area that philosophers would like to examine or study?

As arrogant as it sounds, Philosophers believe that everything can be examined philosophically and there is no issue that cannot be analyzed philosophically. In fact, Philosophers claim that asking a philosophical question is not difficult at all. Accordingly, all we need to do is to ask a very basic or fundamental question about what we want to examine philosophically, such as what is X? or, what is the "nature" of X?

Further, we can ask other philosophical questions, such as, how do we "know" about X in the first place? What constitutes the origin or "being" of X?

Generally speaking, it is very simple to create a new discipline in philosophy as already demonstrated with the above example. Accordingly, the Philosophy of X is concerned with all issues about and related to X.

What is X?
What is the origin of X?
What is the nature of X?

Philosophy of Art (Aesthetics)
This discipline is concerned with what makes an object have aesthetic value. Is it true, as many people say, that beauty is in the eye of the beholder? The central question here is: What is art? What is the criterion for judging that a particular human creation deserves to be called Art?

A NATURALISTIC INTRODUCTION TO PHILOSOPHY

<u>Other Examples:</u> Philosophy of Religion - Philosophy of Religion is concerned with what makes a belief system a religion. Is Scientology a religion? Is Satanism a religion? Why?

<u>Your Comments:</u>

<u>Summary:</u>
There is no specific area of study for Philosophers. Philosophers are interested in all issues, such as morality (ethics), knowledge (epistemology), correct reasoning (logic), social and political Philosophy, and many more.

1. Explain why you believe that Astrology is not considered a science but astronomy is? (Philosophy of Science)

2. Explain why you believe that the *Mona Lisa* should be considered Art? (Philosophy of Art).

3. Explain what all good actions have in common and why? (Moral Philosophy/Ethics).

WHY PHILOSOPHY?
(PURPOSE OF PHILOSOPHY)

In the previous section, it was stated that Philosophers can examine many issues, but it was not stated why these issues should be examined in the first place.

To support his view, Socrates referred to small children who have all kinds of questions on just about every issue. In addition, Socrates believed that asking questions is unavoidable, since life forces us to make a decision or choice once we are confronted with many competing options.

All in all, instead of waiting to have these questions about which option to choose or have them forced upon us, we should ask these questions **before** they arrive and find a justification for them. In this regard, Socrates expressed his famous statement: "The unexamined life is not worth living." Accordingly, we should find a justified account for our lifestyles concerning why we live our lives the way we do, so that we become aware of our conscious decisions and our lives in general.

It may be stated that Socrates intended to inspire people about various issues by provoking or confronting them with his questions, or maybe he simply intended to shake up our minds so that we can "wake up" from our daily routines and become aware of our conscious decisions.

In short, why do we have to engage in a philosophical activity, especially when Philosophers seem to be unable to answer any of these questions definitely or finally (many people believe that the study of Philosophy causes more confusion)?

Is Scientology a religion? Is Satanism a religion? Why?

Scientology Logo

Since Socrates believed that it is natural for humans to ask questions, he believed that philosophizing should not be limited to the professional philosophers, and therefore everyone could and should participate in the critical activity of Philosophy (asking questions).

Socrates

Russell believed that philosophy is there to open our minds by reflecting on various issues. Accordingly, we learn to see "familiar things in an unfamiliar way," and therefore, reflective thinking is the most important contribution or constructive part of practicing philosophy.

Bertrand Russell

A NATURALISTIC INTRODUCTION TO PHILOSOPHY

All things considered, it is difficult to find an agreement among philosophers as far as what philosophy is supposed to accomplish or why practice philosophy at all, partly because each philosopher has his or her own Metaphilosophy, or understanding of Philosophy.

Perhaps it can be stated that if the study of philosophy doesn't help us reach "wisdom" as it was promised by some philosophers in the past, at the minimum it can assist us in recognizing "non-sense" and from there avoid talking "non-sense."

Your Comments:

What do you believe the study of Philosophy can do for you?
Explain your answer in 2 to 3 paragraphs.

A NATURALISTIC INTRODUCTION TO PHILOSOPHY

WHAT METHODS ARE USED IN PHILOSOPHY?

It is safe to say that philosophers universally can agree more on what is, or should be, the subject of philosophy than what should be the method used for addressing philosophical issues.

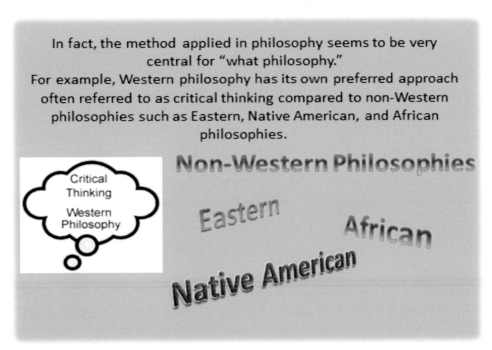

In fact, the method applied in philosophy seems to be very central for "what philosophy."
For example, Western philosophy has its own preferred approach often referred to as critical thinking compared to non-Western philosophies such as Eastern, Native American, and African philosophies.

Critical Thinking
Western Philosophy

Non-Western Philosophies

Eastern

African

Native American

Thinking Critically

Although critical thinking begins with asking questions, it is much more than being skeptical and inquisitive. It means also following the guidelines of logic systematically for challenging claims and ideas in general (see lecture concerning logic).

& Logic Guidelines

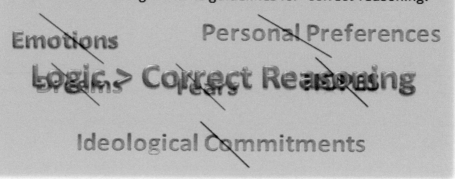

Rational Thinking

While Philosophers have different understandings of what is meant with rational thinking, at the minimum, the notion of being rational, at least historically, means excluding emotions, personal preferences, dreams, hopes, and fears, as well as ideological commitments. In addition, rational thinking requires a commitment to logic and its guidelines for "correct reasoning."

~~Emotions~~   ~~Personal Preferences~~

~~Logic~~ > Correct Reasoning ~~issues~~

~~Ideological Commitments~~

SYSTEMATIC THINKING

Systematic thinking is based on the commitment to connect ideas or to demonstrate the relationship between different components of a theory or a concept.

Mathematical descriptions, for example, are very systematic. Further, rational thinking is also systematic thinking because following a procedure or a method (rational method) is about approaching an issue "step by step." In addition, systematic thinking is partly about being consistent by avoiding contradictions.

Force = mass X acceleration

RATIONAL METHOD

STEP 1

STEP 2

STEP 3

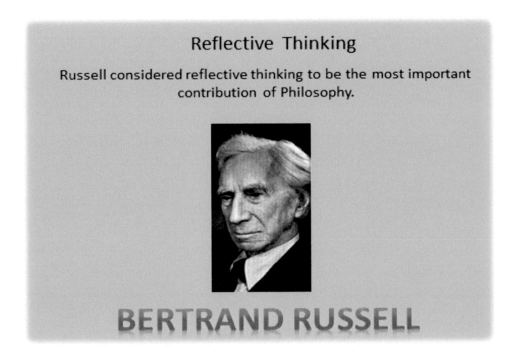

He believed that reflective thinking is important because it opens our minds by helping us "to see familiar things in an unfamiliar way." Reflective thinking is therefore about examining other options, possible solutions, and problems associated with:

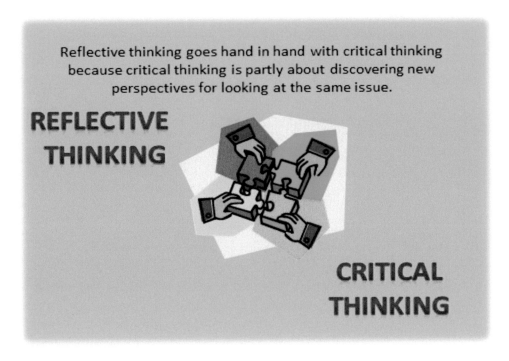

Normative Thinking

Traditional Western Philosophy is normative, which means that Philosophy aims at prescribing truth.

With prescribing truth in this regard is meant that philosophy aims at making JUDGEMENTS about what things OUGHT to be or how things OUGHT to be.

Specifically, philosophy is normative by prescribing, for example, what ought to count as knowledge, real, moral, etc.

Different Styles used in Western Philosophy

There are historically two types of philosophy in the Western tradition. One is known as continental and the other one is known as analytic. It is important to state that the differences are about style as well as the method used for approaching philosophical issues.

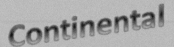

Continental   Analytic

Continental Philosophy

Continental Philosophy gets its name from continental Europe and primarily from central European countries such as France and Germany. This means that historically, German and French Philosophers prefer this type of "doing Philosophy" (practicing Philosophy).

Continental Philosophers such as Nietzsche often use poetic language in their work.
This means that continental philosophers have little commitment to logic and rationality. Just for this reason alone, continental philosophers can be seen as not being systematic in pursuing their agendas and accordingly less critical (not so critical when it comes to challenging ideas and claims).

Friederich Nietzsche

It is a weakness of continental philosophy that the language is not so accessible (sometimes too academic or abstract) and therefore often confusing. Other examples of continental philosophy are Hegel, the French existentialists, and Kierkegaard.

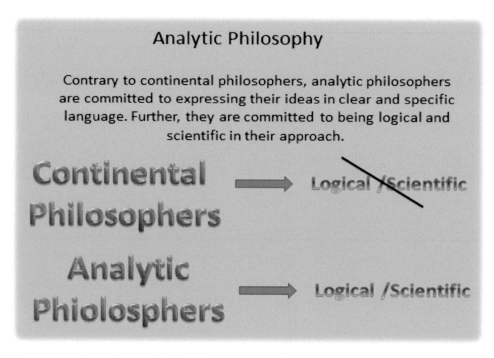

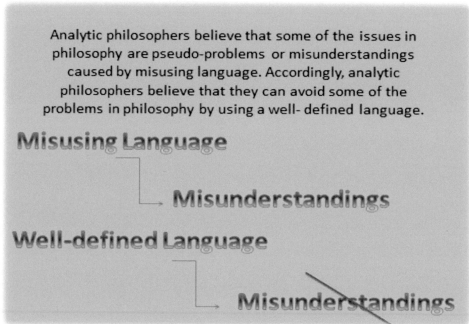

Further, they believe that one must be committed to a specific method or procedure for solving problems in philosophy (for more concerning analytic philosophy, see Descartes's rationalism).

A NATURALISTIC INTRODUCTION TO PHILOSOPHY

Other examples of analytic philosophy are Logical Positivism, Naturalism, and Pragmatism, or any other philosophical view that aims at removing metaphysics or minimizing the influence of metaphysics on philosophical discourses.

Your Comments:

Test your knowledge:

1. What is meant by critical thinking?

2.Explain why analytic philosophy is more critical than continental philosophy.

3. What do you think if one claims that religious views are not reflective and therefore not critical?

Metaphilosophical differences between Western and non-Western Philosophies

Western Philosophy is characterized, at least historically, by its repeated commitment to differentiate between philosophy and religion.

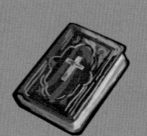

Accordingly, philosophical activities are critical while religious activities are not. This means that philosophical views are not based on "faith" or "trust," while this is precisely the case with religious beliefs.

Further, religious beliefs are not critical because there is often an authority such as a prophet who tells the truth and demands acceptance or trust in return, which means that you accept uncritically (without any questions or any other form of challenge) what you are told.

Contrary to this, non-Western Philosophies often discuss philosophy and religion in the same context (philosophy participates in solving religious problems / religions generate issues for philosophical investigations).

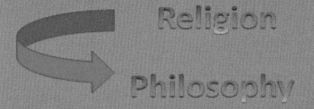 

This means that there is no separation between philosophy and religion, and therefore both merge into one interdisciplinary project (one cannot tell where religion ends and where philosophy begins, and vice versa).

Other differences between Western and non-Western Philosophies

A.
Non-Western philosophies emphasize the intimate relationship between philosophy and life, which means that non-Western philosophies are concerned with practical applications of philosophy to life.

This means that any philosophical activity is a practical activity and its result or truth is tangible, while in the Western tradition philosophical activities are primarily presented as mere intellectual exercises with <u>possible</u> practical applications in life, such as seeking wisdom, avoiding ignorance, etc.

Non-Western   Western

→ Practical Activity

B.
Non-Western philosophies are often concerned with human nature and its place in the world as well as "the human inner world" (state of the human spirit),.......

......while Western philosophy has a long history of being concerned with the outer world or the external world (what is distinct from humans).

Another way of explaining the difference is to say that the truth that western Philosophy often looks for is "non-human truth," or so-called "objective truth," while the type of truth that non-Western Philosophies aim at discovering (identifying) is "human truth," such as subjective truth (personal truth) and inter-subjective (social / cultural) truth.

Objective Truth

versus

Subjective Truth

This historical tendency in Western philosophy, namely to search for non-human truth, can be seen as one factor among many others that could explain the fascination of Western cultures with "objectivity," and with that, the emergence of natural sciences in Western civilization. Accordingly, the natural sciences originated mainly in Western cultures partly because of their tendency to look for non-human truth which is external or natural (objective) and not internal (personal) nor social.

Geology

Astronomy

Biology

C.

Western philosophical views are based on the understanding that the knowing subject (human) is distinct from the object of knowledge (world). This separation between the subject and the object provides the foundation for many theories of knowledge that have been developed in Western cultures.

These theories of knowledge are called representative theories of knowledge, because the relationship between the knowing subject and the object known can be imagined as a relationship that is assumed between a "representation" that exists as a state of consciousness in the mind of the knowing subject (for example in your mind) and a thing (object represented) which exist in the outside world or external world (the world distinct from your mind).

Representations of wheels in the Mind   A Monster truck in the outside world

Based on the above example, the wheels of the truck are being represented in the mind. It is important to note that with "representation" in Western epistemology is meant a mental representation which is nothing but a state of awareness present in the mind, such as your memory of a past experience.

Contrary to the above-described Western view, there is no separation between the knowing subject and object known. Based on many non-Western philosophical views, the subject and object can be united, and this unity or "oneness" explains how non-Western philosophical views integrate religious experiences into their philosophy, and philosophy into religion.

Philosophy

Religion

Accordingly, the knowing subject can be united with nature / spirit or God, and consequently non-Western philosophies often encourage spirituality or oneness of man with Nature / spirit / God.

Further, since non-Western philosophies preferably have an inward- and not an outward- looking approach (as it is in Western philosophy), non-Western philosophical views often study various states of human spiritual existence and therefore aim at improving human spiritual destiny as an important purpose of their philosophical activities or projects. Example:

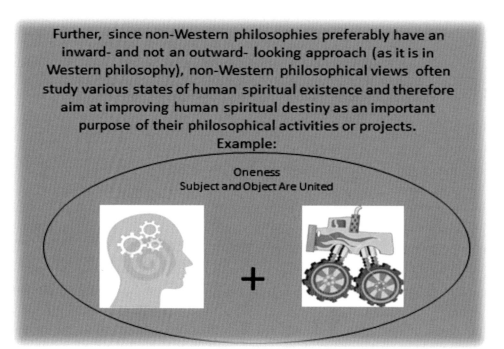

Buddhism is an example of a non-Western philosophy that often promotes the "oneness" in the above described meaning. Other examples are Native American philosophy or even Islamic Philosophy (Irfan as the linguistic science of mystical apprehension encourages "oneness" or unicity as described above).

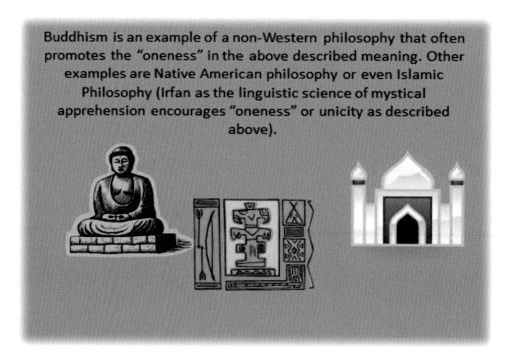

All things considered, it is safe to say that it is characteristic for many non-Western philosophies to promote a holistic approach for philosophical investigations due to the belief that we (humans) are part of the world and not distinct from it, and consequently, seeking objectivity is a myth of Western cultures and not actually obtainable.

Your Comments:

Test your knowledge:

1. What is the main methodological difference between Western and non-Western philosophies?

2. Do you agree with non-Western philosophies using spiritual experiences as methods for gathering knowledge? Explain why.

NATURALISTIC PHILOSOPHY

Since philosophy is not there to compete with science or replace science, it makes sense to include scientific knowledge in our philosophical discourses. For example, how can philosophy investigate reality or the world of our daily experience without including the reality that sciences have revealed to us the subatomic world and the macro cosmos—the universe—that is approximately 13.8 billion years old?

In general, what is the relationship between science and philosophy? And if science and philosophy are complementary how much science, if any, should be involved in philosophical investigations?

Above all, why shouldn't we have science in philosophy? Why shouldn't we take advantage of scientific knowledge that is already there?

As we will see later, Naturalism as a philosophical view has its own metaphilosophy or understanding of subject, method, and purpose of philosophy. But to introduce this philosophy for the first time, it is pedagogically more effective to begin with what is known as "naturalistic epistemology" or "epistemology naturalized." This type of epistemology is the theory of knowledge that is applied and presupposed by naturalists.

WHAT IS MEANT BY EPISTEMOLOGY NATURALIZED?

The epistemology of naturalism not only aims at using scientific knowledge, but it also takes advantage of scientific method and procedure. For example, a naturalized epistemology is an attempt to bring psychology or any other science into epistemology and vice versa, to integrate epistemology into science.

The difference between traditional philosophy and naturalistic philosophy is that while non-naturalists question whether continuity between epistemology and science actually exists or is possible, naturalists presuppose this with their questions—for instance, how humans arrive at factual knowledge, including how the reliability of such knowledge can be explained scientifically.

According to Friedman (1979), "Naturalism seeks to derive the reliability of our methods from our psychological and physical theories, our theories about how the human mind arrives at beliefs through interaction with its environment."

In search of an empirical account (a posteriori), naturalists aim not only at defining but also solving epistemological problems in terms of scientific problems. They aim at adopting scientific methods and knowledge for dealing with epistemological issues. Although consistency with science is a necessary condition, James Maffie (1990) proposes six forms of continuity between epistemology and science as sufficient conditions.

CONTEXTUAL CONTINUITY

Contextual continuity means that naturalists reject non-contextualism, which equates with the understanding that epistemological activities must be pursued contextually and specifically in the context of science. In other words, epistemological activities occur as scientific activities. Therefore epistemological issues and problems are defined and answered scientifically in accordance with the very same framework that scientists use to pursue their agendas. As Maffie states, "Naturalists maintain that epistemology takes place within the context of natural sciences. It occurs as an enterprise within science, neither coming before nor standing outside of science."

EPISTEMOLOGICAL CONTINUITY

Epistemological continuity means that epistemological issues, such as skepticism, will be addressed a posteriori as well. It determines whether knowledge about the external world is possible or not. Epistemological continuity also means that questions concerning knowledge production must be empirical questions, and therefore epistemology no longer operates a priori in regulating beliefs. As Maffie puts it, "Naturalized epistemology thus moves away from claims of special evidence, be it divine, a priori, scriptural, or the dictates of pure reason."

METHODOLOGICAL CONTINUITY

Methodological continuity is continuity in method between epistemology and science. The procedures for gathering knowledge in the sciences are the same as the procedures in epistemology. According to Maffie (1990), "Naturalized epistemology employs ordinary scientific methods (e.g., observation, testing, induction, experimentation) in resolving problems." Methodological continuity further claims that epistemology loses its self-proclaimed superiority in approach for prescribing truth, including which type of knowledge is more dependable as well as how knowledge should be developed.

ANALYTIC CONTINUITY

Analytic continuity is continuity in language between epistemology and science. Maffie interprets analytic continuity as "analyzing, explicating, reducing epistemological concepts in terms of purely descriptive concepts, predicates and assertions." In this regard, the school of Naturalism that aims at removing the normativity of epistemology entirely adopts the language and style of descriptive sciences completely. Adopting such language might include expressing hypothetical assertions that are true conditionally, as is common in scientific studies, rather than language that is concerned with establishing a state of affairs through arguments and demonstrations.

METAPHYSICAL CONTINUITY

Metaphysical continuity means establishing metaphysical continuity between the objects in epistemology and objects in science. Maffie (1990) describes metaphysical continuity as "Epistemic properties, facts, or states of affairs that are to be argued, to be identical with, constituted by, or supervenient upon descriptive properties, facts, or states of affairs." Since irrealist (anti-realist) accounts can establish the metaphysical continuity between epistemology and science more successfully than realist accounts can, naturalism supports irrealism rather than realism.

AXIOLOGICAL CONTINUITY

Axiological continuity means that the inquiry concerning epistemic ends and norms must be conducted a posteriori. Further, the rules for justification must be examined in terms of their utility promoting epistemic ends. Maffie (1990) states, "The epistemic ends are grounded in facts about ourselves (e.g., our contingent desires, what it is for us to desire something, etc.), our environment, and how our actions affect our ability to realize our desires." In short, axiological continuity is that as far as what is to be desired and valued are to be determined a posteriori and not presupposed a priori (e.g., self-evident Kantian axiology of his enlightenment project such as the notion of "pure reason").

Chapter 2
Critical Thinking

HOW TO PRESENT A PHILOSOPHICAL IDEA CRITICALLY

Philosophizing (actively participating in developing or constructing a philosophical idea) is no different than presenting a philosophical idea or evaluating someone's philosophical views due to philosophy in general. It must be treated critically.

Practicing philosophy critically means that one examines the language and the method applied by the philosopher closely and carefully. Accordingly, the philosopher must introduce the key terms and concepts carefully; they must be defined clearly.

Although conceptual analyzes is not the final or the only objective of philosophy, linguistic analyses are mandatory for any constructive way of discussing philosophy. When a philosopher uses an academic term, he or she must tell us how he understands them, in which context he is entitled to use them and why.

The danger of not practicing philosophy systematically is that philosophy can quickly turn into a performing-arts activity if the sole purpose becomes presenting an idea in its complete version with great enthusiasm, leaving students with nothing but the impression that the teacher is knowledgeable, competent, or a good communicator. . . .

All things considered, the philosophers are obligated to work methodically and systematically in their approaches, and, as has already been said, we need to be told from the beginning what method the philosopher aims to apply, where the argument is, where the premises are, and ultimately how these ideas have matured in to the concepts or ideas that the philosopher intends to establish (justify) or promote. In other words, the chain of thoughts and their evolution must be demonstrated clearly and carefully, step-by-step, so that everyone can understand how this or that proposal has originated and has been further developed.

What is particularly crucial for the Western tradition is that practicing philosophy critically requires that ideas are sophisticated enough to defend themselves, and they don't depend on constant care, including ad hoc explanations or any other form of external help such as authorities.

In summary, a philosophical idea that is presented critically offers enough transparency, allowing everyone to verify and evaluate the validity of the claims, supporting arguments, and the explanations associated with them.

WHAT IS MEANT BY CRITICAL THINKING?

While many faculty members emphasize the importance of critical thinking, they don't teach how to think critically. What has been often overlooked is that critical thinking requires knowledge but also familiarity with certain methods and procedures. The question therefore becomes what method/ procedure to use.

Thinking critically begins with thinking independently. As obvious as this might seem, it is overlooked that thinking independently requires acting freely from other people's pressures, rewards, and approvals as well as other manipulative attempts.

This is an important aspect to consider due to us humans who are often influenced by our surrounding culture, social interests, and interactions with our friends and family members, and it is rare that we are willing to take the risk of stressing these relationships that we strongly care about. Precisely speaking, because of these personal concerns (psychological nature), most individuals, if they were honest, would confess that too often they are guilty of following their loved ones blindly due to their concern of protecting these relationships and the people that they care about. This is a much greater desire than the desire to seek truth.

Historically, critical thinking is a characteristic of Western tradition, while this tradition is based on a non-holistic worldview or metaphysics, presupposing the distinction between the message and the messenger. In accordance with this tradition, thinking critically is only about the message but not the messenger, which is to say one ought to challenge and examine the merit of an idea in isolation and NOT in relation to the person or people who believe in these ideas. Ignoring the messenger and strictly focusing on the ideas or belief itself prevents an informal fallacy known as ad hominem fallacy (argument the person fallacy).

Again, this separation is supposed to prevent evaluating an argument based on who is defending it. In this regard, even a "bad person" or criminal or someone unexperienced, and the like, could have a good idea or a valid point.

Another aspect that is worth serious consideration is that thinking critically often leads to unintentionally offending someone. This way of thinking will unavoidably turn into questioning or challenging an idea, a belief, or values that one might feel strongly about. But should this concern that we potentially offend someone prevent us from a debate or discussion about certain issues? Should this concern limit or even deter us from thinking critically?

This might be the only instance (searching for truth using critical thinking) in which the feelings should not matter or should not be considered at all, not even when we offend our loved ones. Unfortunately, it seems that this is what it takes to search for truth, namely demonstrating the courage to question authorities and institutions that are well respected socially and culturally as well as taking the risk of offending or disrespecting people that we care about.

I mentioned "courage" due to awareness that offending some institutions and authorities could bring repercussions for the critical thinker, but in spite of social isolation, ridicule, and backlash, one must be willing to pay the price needed for examining issues nevertheless. The story of Socrates is the best historical example for what could happen to any individual who shows the courage and dares examining status quo and other established norms regardless of what thinking critically might lead to and what outcome it might generate.

In short, "be careful what you wish for" definitely applies to critical thinking because wishing for the truth might bring regrets and sorrow.

POSITIVE AND NEGATIVE DEFINITIONS OF THINKING CRITICALLY

As stated above, thinking critically requires examining all the details involved, including the definitions that philosophers have used to present their ideas (as people say, "the devil is in the details"). This is especially true for practicing philosophy analytically. Analytic philosophy demands even more attention to the use of language and other details such as key assumptions and concepts presupposed as well as definitions.

In philosophy, there are various kinds of definitions: Negative, Positive, Descriptive, and Normative.

Negative Definitions: X is defined negatively if we are told what X is not. The Negative definitions are used to exclude certain qualities/properties. For example, a car is not a bicycle but a car is also not an airplane or a train or a house.

The use of Negative definitions should be avoided as much as possible because they do not clarify or explain much in spite of their popularity among philosophers such as Aristotle. The negative definitions could be used as stepping-stones to reach a higher degree of clarity, as it is the case with affirmative explanations, but philosophers often get stuck with the negative definitions that they introduce originally, failing to make the transition in to positive definitions.

Positive Definitions: Positive Definitions are the type of definitions that we all expect to have. Positive definitions affirm something such as what X is or has or can do. These types of definitions clarify and explain a quality or property of something. For example, a triangle has three sides.

Descriptive Definitions: These types of definitions describe how things are, how something is used, how X as an activity is practiced, applied, understood by most people/members of a culture, and so on. The descriptive definitions might also clarify the context or the situation under which a term is applicable. Most scientific definitions are in fact descriptive such as water is a liquid that freezes at 0 degrees Celsius.

Normative definitions: The Normative definitions concern how things ought to be or ought to be understood or ought to be applied, practiced, and so on.

Some scientific definitions are normative such as a healthy person has a 97 degree temperature. Normative definitions are conventional and therefore often demanded by cultures and institutions to follow policies and procedures.

Negative definition of Critical Thinking: A negative definition of critical thinking would only assert what thinking critically is NOT rather than what it is. Nevertheless, through exclusions, a negative definition can point out certain common mistakes (fallacies) that one should avoid to enhance critical-thinking skills. For example, adopting a sheep mentality (following the crowd blindly), also known as appealing to people indirectly, is not critical.

Generally speaking, it is very demanding for most people to avoid fallacies (mistakes in reasoning) because humans as social beings have strong psychological desires for feeling accepted, appreciated, recognized, and, in general, valued by the culture or subculture they belong to.

Another common mistake influencing our critical-thinking ability is when an idea is proposed by a famous person or an authority. For example, Plato said so . . . , or the prophet said once . . . , or our president demanded. . . .

The point to notice here is that celebrity status or fame does not prove or establish anything, but since the majority of people feel intimidated by authorities, there is a tendency among people to outsource their thinking to "experts." Of course there are areas that we do have experts or we need and depend on experts opinion, such as doing a surgery in hospital or flying an airplane, but there are no experts for everyday life issues or many other areas of human life that require critical-thinking skills.

Having said that, there have been many mass manipulators in the history of various cultures who have presented themselves as "experts," and it is partly the social political task of the critical thinker to identify these charlatans and expose them.

In this regard, there is another psychological factor that often interferes with our judgments and thinking in general. That is when an idea is presented with a great level of confidence by, for instance, politicians, preachers, and demagogues in history (such as Hitler) who succeeded solely because they presented their ideas with "style" (a great level of confidence). And we all know based on experience that the confidence level of the speaker is perhaps the most important psychological factor that can influence or convince the audience. As people sometimes say: "He knows what he is talking about," meaning that he must be right simply because the idea is presented with high confidence.

With all things considered, there are many other psychological tricks, also known as informal fallacies, that demagogues have been using and they continue to use such as appeal to fear (e.g., the straw man argument, red herring, begging the question fallacy, etc.) to sell their ideologies and or secure their personal, national, or cultural interests. Having knowledge of these fallacies allows identifying their presence in a discussion, and with that it increases the effectiveness of thinking.

Your Comments:

POSITIVE AND DESCRIPTIVE DEFINITIONS OF CRITICAL THINKING

It should not be overlooked that thinking critically is a cultural activity, and logic is a very important part of it. The essential point here is that thinking critically is not just about being logical, although logic provides important guidelines and methods for thinking "correctly" (more on that later in this chapter). What should be highlighted is that any critical approach uses and presupposes many psychological activities that are as crucial as the coherent guidelines of formal logic.

For example, the factor "courage" as it was discussed earlier, requires that one overcome fear of challenging authorities and mainstream beliefs. In such a context, what makes critical thinking "scary" to some people is that they have to consider the possibility of being on the wrong side of an issue. When Socrates stated that "the unexamined life is not worth living," he meant that one ought to question his/her own lifestyle, beliefs, choices, and values because to most people it comes very naturally to question other people's beliefs and choices, but the challenge associated with being critical is that one is questioning his/her own views. The self-talk associated with this process would be like this: Maybe I am wrong; maybe I misjudged, underestimated, overinterpreted, and so on.

It is understandable for most people to admit mistakes or even consider the possibility that they were wrong (have lived their lives believing in wrong things and having wrong values), but as stated before, this is the risk and sacrifice involved in seeking truth.

Another psychological condition for thinking critically is the willingness to be moved by reason. If the parties involved are not willing to accept any argument or evidence whatsoever, then there is no chance for having a constructive discussion.

The purpose of being engaged in any critical activity, including philosophical activity, is to seek clarity or search for some truth and not to entertain. Discussing philosophy only for the sake of having a discussion has no academic value and ultimately leads to nothing but a waste of time even if it amuses participants in the process.

Generally speaking, philosophical debates have no chance to succeed if they are not structured, methodic, and systematic. It is therefore no surprise that people engaged in social political or religious debates often end the discussions with bitterness and anger. For example, if truth types and truth concepts of participants are different—or participants are not aware of their own assumptions, arguments, methods, and beliefs—any discussion of this sort is doomed to fail. In other words, any non-structured and ill-prepared discussion can only get emotional and frustrating and end with no tangible results.

Although most people are not equipped with the necessary tools mentioned above, nor are they reflective or serious enough to take the time and effort to prepare for a critical discussion, at minimum we have to bring some integrity into our daily debates if we want the discussion to get somewhere. By integrity, I mean the willingness to be moved by reason; participants ought to be psychologically strong enough to change their views/opinions if a better argument or some other form of justification (scientific, for example) is presented by their opponents.

47

In the absence of integrity, debates have no chance of becoming fruitful since participants are not really listening to and evaluating ideas but instead are focused on what they need to say next to "win the debate" or change the view of their opponents. (I strongly discourage people to be engaged in such debates since the original mission, such as searching for truth or seeking clarity and the like, is actually replaced by a game that is entirely useless and meaningless.)

Among all the above-mentioned obstacles facing the critical thinker, there is another difficulty that cannot remain unnoticed. Thinking critically requires impartiality, but humans are extremely partial beings and we all know from our experience that we always prefer our loved ones and family members over strangers. Now as critical thinkers we are challenged by the demand that we ought to exclude personal interests and social, cultural, religious, and political commitments as well as other biases as much as possible. In this regard, it is legitimate to ask if it is even realistic to ask humans to shut down all of their emotions and preferences by being entirely objective and unbiased. The answer to this question is yes and no, because on one side humans cannot be entirely unbiased no matter how hard they try and on the other side, it is appropriate in the context of critical thinking to at least try to be as unbiased and objective as one is capable.

For example, consider judges who are asked to be unbiased. Certainly, it is difficult for some of them (occasionally) to exclude their preferences all the time but <u>this is what it takes to be a judge</u>. It is expected from judges to be objective and at least it is expected from them to give their best when they interpret the law, regardless of social, cultural, political, and other associations of the person who is on trial. Similarly, a critical thinker should free himself/-herself from all political tendencies, hopes, wishes, dreams, fears, cultural associations, and so on when he or she is engaged in a serious academic debate or investigation.

Finally, since academic integrity is essential for being a true investigator in philosophy, it would make sense to admit (at least sometimes) that some questions must remain unanswered for now till we have more knowledge. In other words, the critical thinker is able to live with the anxiety of not knowing, which demands some mental strength. Some individuals must have an answer for every question, and they believe that having some answer is better than having no answer at all, but in the context of critical thinking the notion that a bad answer is better than the state of not knowing is a wrong choice. In fact, a false belief can create an illusion, and a sense of false security can be more deceptive and harder to overcome than not having any ideas at all.

Let's consider this analogy: You are hungry and there are two options available to you. On one side you have the option of eating a food that is very old and potentially dangerous and the other option would be to stay hungry and tolerate the pain of feeling hungry. What would you do? Perhaps the option of not eating the rotten food is a healthier and safer choice in the long run than the option of eating food that has gone bad, in spite of temporarily eliminating the pain of staying hungry.

In summary, in spite of the fact that it might be difficult for one to tolerate the state of not knowing, one can learn to live with it or get used to it. Accordingly, the willingness to hold final judgment in abeyance is an indispensable or vital requirement for thinking critically.

The last aspect of critical thinking that will be discussed here briefly is that being critical requires some humility. Humility is the willingness to accept constructive criticism. Not taking things personally and welcoming feedback is vital for enhancing thoughts, proposals, and theories that one is working on or interested in developing further. For example, publishing an article or a book in philosophy but not hearing back from academicians is not a good sign since it would only suggest that the work was not worthy of a critical examination or any serious academic evaluation. To appreciate constructive criticism in the world of academia, one has to learn not to personalize professional ideas or beliefs by creating a distance between these ideas and the one who is presenting them. In the absence of such a distance, ideas defended or promoted turn quickly in-to propaganda or something else. Therefore it is the responsibility of the critical thinker not to feel attached to any belief or concept since emotional attachments would also compromise future investigations and reevaluations of ideas.

What is noticeable so far is that critical thinking comes with its own psychological conditions or its own mind-set, including its unique attitude toward the world of experience and available interpretations of this world that surrounds us.

Let's reiterate and emphasize this again: The objective of practicing philosophy as a critical activity neither is nor should be to come up with a bulletproof ideology (best possible ideology) that is eternal, unchanging, and universally valid for all humanity. Instead, it is far more about sharpening the method of investigating and searching various ideas without any commitment to what the final result must "look like." It is to underline that even the method of investigation and inquiry that is being "enhanced" over time neither is nor should be final, and hence it will be subject to change and modified and eventually replaced.

With all things considered, a philosopher is a critical thinker who welcomes criticism that would allow him/her to develop ideas further. Since philosophy is critical and it is not based on faith or trust, the philosopher should not be afraid of realizing that his ideas including his/her long dearly held beliefs turn out to be false.

Practicing philosophy is like finding yourself in a maze. Once determined that a route leads to nowhere, it must be abandoned so that other routes get a chance for success.

At the end, it is ironic to ask why philosophers struggle so much to let go (Plato's ontological dualism, for example) and, above all, why scientists are not so attached to their beliefs as much as philosophers are. Does it mean that scientists practice critical thinking better than the philosophers do?

BEING CRITICAL ABOUT STATEMENTS:
DIFFERENCES BETWEEN EMOTIVE AND COGNITIVE STATEMENTS

Could we have "progress" in philosophy as there is progress in science? The answer to this question depends on whether philosophers have learned from the history of philosophy by avoiding certain mistakes or not. One lesson that philosophers should have learned from the history of philosophy is that we CANNOT be critical about every statement. Some statements, for example, are classified as emotive, such as I prefer chocolate ice cream, or I prefer to spend my summer vacation at the beach. These statements lack truth value, meaning that they have neither true truth value nor false truth value, hence they cannot be subject of critical analyses.

The Emotive statements are called emotive because they are expressions of feelings and therefore are subjective in a sense that they apply to conditions or interests of only one individual or person. It is noteworthy that poetic statements are also emotive since they are expressions of poets wondering about…

On the other side, there are cognitive statements. These types of statements have truth values, meaning that they are either true or false, such as factual statements or scientific statements. Now since descriptive statements are factual in a sense that they express a state of affairs, they can be true or false and hence cognitive.

Generally speaking, objective claims, such as how things are or how things work in the world/nature, are factual and therefore have cognitive meaning and are worthy of critical analyses. For example, the earth is not flat. This statement is a factual claim or an objective claim about the shape of our planet and it does not communicate anyone's preference or feeling.

Unfortunately, philosophers for a long time didn't pay attention to the use of language and the problems associated with it. Thanks to the contributions of logical positivism at the beginning of the twentieth century, the importance and relevance of language became clear. Especially A. J. Ayer in his famous work *Language, Truth and Logic* (1936) demonstrated how philosophers, and metaphysicians in particular, were sloppy and careless with the use of language and as a result, they became confused about the types of their claims and the statements expressing them. Accordingly, often philosophers simply expressed their preferred interpretations or personal views of the world (subjective claims) while they falsely classified and presented these subjective expressions as factual statements with objective claims. The point is that one cannot be critical about these statements (about people's feelings such as I am cold or I am hungry).

Finally, it must be stated at this point that factual statements should be determined scientifically and not philosophically. Although philosophy is critical about objective claims as well as sciences, sciences are equipped with methods and procedures that are more capable of testing/examining the truth and falsity of factual or objective claims, including verification or confirmation of the truth value of objective claims.

Revisiting the original question asked concerning the possibility of making progress in philosophy, it can be stated now that it is NOT the task of philosophy to compete with science or to replace science. Accordingly, all factual claims concerning the natural world and human existence as biological beings should be left to sciences and not to philosophy.

But what would be the contribution of philosophy in this context? What is there left to be accomplished philosophically? The answer is that the purpose of philosophy is to lay out the foundation for formulating questions that are factual and demand factual answers with objective claims. In other words, the purpose of philosophy is to prepare a path or stepping-stones needed for creating sciences, including a critical framework under which sciences originate and evolve. This is the contribution of philosophy, which is part of the process of so-called naturalistic project (see chapter 4, Epistemology, concerning this topic).

DIFFERENCES BETWEEN ARGUMENTS AND EXPLANATIONS

In a critical context, one is not allowed to claim, propose, and demand actions unless these claims and ideas are established with an argument. Presenting an argument is the standard method of reasoning for justifying claims in philosophy.

In fact, the strength of a philosophical work is determined partly on how well an idea is established (how strong the supporting arguments are). Strictly speaking, arguments provide the evidence needed to accept certain views or proposals, such as if something is true, real, or moral.

While arguments justify claims, explanations describe how things are and how things change, interact, originate. It is noteworthy that explanations don't prove anything, no matter how long or detailed or sophisticated they are, therefore it is crucial to distinguish between arguments and explanations. Explanations as descriptions only clarify what is already accepted as knowledge, real, moral, and so on. For example, it is the primary function of a scientific theory to provide explanations concerning how things change in nature, how physical events are linked or can be predicted and controlled. In short, while arguments justify if things are this or that, explanations describe how things are/how things work.

DIFFERENCES BETWEEN SCIENTIFIC AND PHILOSOPHICAL JUSTIFICATIONS

The difference between philosophical and scientific justification is extremely important for everyday debates and discussions. If one is asking for proof, the first response should be "what currency do you accept?" meaning what kind of proof do you accept, scientific or philosophical?

As stated above, normative claims are established or proven using arguments, while descriptive claims of science are established or proven using experiments. An experiment is a systematic method of observing/predicting a process. Experiments are a standard method of justification for natural sciences such as physics, chemistry, and biology. These sciences not only develop their knowledge methodically through experiments, but they also use experiments for the confirmation of any particular knowledge.

As it was stated in the previous chapter, naturalistic views or interpretations require that the so-called standard method of justification (arguments) is replaced with standard scientific justifications of science (experiments). For more on this topic see chapter 4 concerning Epistemology naturalized.

Your Comments:

LOGIC

The Importance of Logic

The importance of logic, at least in the Western tradition, can be summarized by saying that the strength of a philosophical idea depends on the sophistication of an argument or reasoning that supports it.

This means that without logic, it is impossible to determine which idea is correct and which idea is not (it cannot be determined who makes sense and who doesn't).

Which Idea is Worth nurturing?

Accordingly, logic assists us not only in evaluating other people's arguments but also helps us develop better, stronger arguments in general.

In other words, the aim of logic is to develop a method for evaluating and analyzing arguments. Specifically, the purpose of logic consists of establishing a reliable method by which we can distinguish between good and bad arguments, strong and weak, valid and invalid.

Argument

Unlike how the term "argument" is used in our daily life, in logic the term "argument" has nothing to do with "having a disagreement or an unpleasant experience with someone." In logic, an argument is a group of statements in which some statements, known as premises, provide support for another statement known as a conclusion.

Premises

support

Conclusion

While the conclusion is the statement that contains a claim saying something is the case, such as X exists or X is true, premises are statements that provide support for the conclusion. One can also say that premises provide the evidence needed to establish the conclusion.

Premises

Evidence

Conclusion

EVALUATING ARGUMENTS

To evaluate an argument, it is better to work systematically since we are unable to evaluate all aspects of an argument all at once.

The first step for evaluating an argument is to assume that the premises are true. (It is notable that a statement can have either a true truth value or a false truth value, and the assumption that the premises are true does not mean that the premises are "really" true.) This allows us to make a judgment about the truth value of the conclusion (amount of support provided for the conclusion).

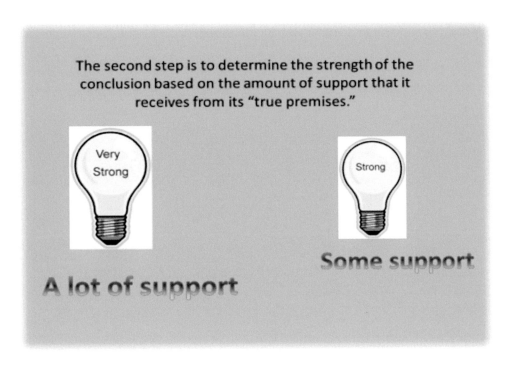

> Generally speaking, the strength of an argument is determined in logic by classifying an argument under different classes, such as inductive, deductive, cogent, sound and unsound, etc. These classifications are part of the method that logic prescribes for evaluating arguments.

CLASSIFYING ARGUMENTS AS INDUCTIVE AND DEDUCTIVE

To classify an argument as inductive or deductive, it is important to assume that the premises are true (the first step). As already stated, by assuming that the premises are true, the truth value of the conclusion can be determined.

> In a case where the conclusion is necessarily true, once we assume that the premises are true the argument is classified as deductive, and in a case where the conclusion can be true or false while the premises are assumed to be true, the argument is classified as inductive.

Deductive ?

Inductive?

In summary, based on the ASSUMPTION that the premises are true, there is a probability or chance that the conclusion is true (inductive reasoning), and based on the ASSUMPTION that the premises are true and the conclusion must be true, the argument is deductive (deductive reasoning).

Assumed True Premises

Inductive Reasoning

Probable True Conclusion

Assumed True Premises

Deductive Reasoning

Conclusion Must be True

Example for deductive reasoning:
Premise1: Baltimore is in Maryland

Premise2: Maryland is in the U.S

Conclusion : Baltimore is in the U.S

Based on the first premise, that Baltimore is in Maryland, and based on the second premise, that Maryland is in the U.S, the conclusion that Baltimore is in the U.S is unavoidably true because it is impossible for Baltimore to be in Maryland and Maryland in the U.S., and at the same time for Baltimore to not be in the U.S.

A similar example would be that 3 is a higher number than 2 and 2 is a higher number than 1, therefore 3 must be a higher number than 1.

Example of inductive reasoning:

Premise 1: Baltimore is in the U.S.
Premise 2: Maryland is in the U.S.
Conclusion: Baltimore is in Maryland

The first premise states that Baltimore is in the U.S., but we are not told exactly where in the U.S. The second premise states that Maryland is in the U.S., and again we are not told where in the U.S., but the conclusion claims that Baltimore must be in Maryland.

By evaluating this argument, we can clearly state that both Baltimore and Maryland can be in the U.S. without Baltimore being in Maryland.

The main issue that one must pay attention to is that when we evaluate an argument, we have to disregard our knowledge about Baltimore, Maryland and the U.S. Our knowledge is limited to what we are told by the premises. Accordingly, we ignore our knowledge that Baltimore really is in Maryland.

Proceeding methodically as described above, the conclusion of the second example can be true or false, which means that the argument is to be classified as inductive.

Assumed True Premises

Inductive Reasoning

Probable True Conclusion

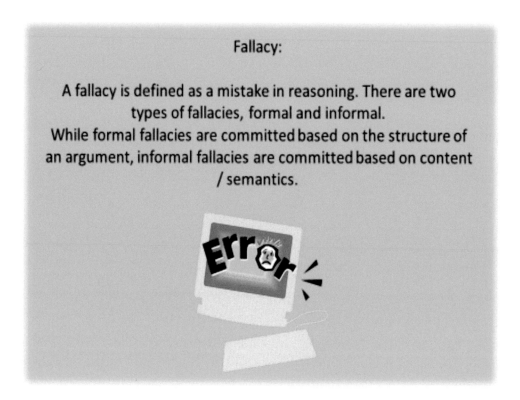

In accordance with the distinction between inductive and deductive arguments, we have "inductive and deductive logic." Unfortunately most arguments developed in Philosophy and in Science are inductive, but mathematical arguments are deductive, including arguments developed in geometry, algebra, and trigonometry.

VALID ARGUMENT FORMS

Often specific deductive argument forms are used to establish ideas. These argument forms are also known as valid argument forms, which are useful tools that can be applied to various occasions to enhance the quality of reasoning.

1. Modus Ponens (MP):   If P, then Q
P

Q

2. Modus Tollens (MT):   If P, then Q
Not Q

Not P

3. Hypothetical Syllogism (HS):   If P, then Q
If Q, then R

If P, then R

4. Disjunctive Syllogism: (DS):   Either P or Q
Not P

Q

(A syllogism is a deductive argument with two premises and one conclusion. All the above arguments are deductively valid.)

A NATURALISTIC INTRODUCTION TO PHILOSOPHY

Test your knowledge:

1.   What is the purpose of Logic?

2. What is an Argument?

3. What is the difference between inductive and deductive arguments?

Homework:

Participate in discussions about the following two arguments. Decide whether these arguments are inductive or deductive and why.

P1. Socrates was Greek. (premise)
P2. Most Greeks eat fish. (premise)
C: Socrates ate fish. (conclusion)

P1. All men are mortal. (premise)
P2. Socrates was a man. (premise)
C: Socrates was mortal. (conclusion)

Your Comments:

Chapter 3
Ethics (Moral Philosophy)

INTRODUCTION TO MORAL STUDIES

Ethics, or moral Philosophy, is the study of principles prescribing human actions in terms of their rightness and wrongness. Ethics is therefore concerned with human behavior, choices, reactions to "serious human problems," and so on. In this context, it is to ask: What would be the difference between ethics and psychology since psychology is also concerned with human behavior, actions, and choices?

DIFFERENCES BETWEEN PSYCHOLOGY AND ETHICS

Perhaps the shortest answer to this question concerning the differences between psychology and ethics would be that while Psychology is descriptive, Ethics is normative. Specifically, ethics is interested in normative issues. Ethics examines moral problems like abortion, euthanasia, DNA research, genetic manipulation, and so on.

Generally speaking, theoretical ethics is pursuing two objectives:

1. To develop ethical theories that can define and justify moral duties of individuals. This objective is about how individuals ought to treat one another and what they ought to do as moral agents.
2. To solve ethical issues. This objective of ethics is concerned with already existing moral problems as well future emerging ones. The goal is, ideally, to solve these problems once, for all in a morally responsible way.

ETHICAL ISSUES

The question of what constitutes an ethical dilemma is identical with what makes a problem ethical. The answer to these questions would also clarify the differences between social political issues and ethical issues.

A NATURALISTIC INTRODUCTION TO PHILOSOPHY

The characteristic for classifying a problem as ethical is that ethical issues are problems that represent conflict of <u>values</u>.

REALISM VS. ANTI-REALISM IN ETHICS

The discussion between Realism and Anti-realism is concerned with the origin of moral truth. In general, this is a metaphysical question about the nature of morality including what constitutes rightness and wrongness in ethics. Mortal realism claims that moral truth exists independently from human culture and existence. In other words, morality is not man-made and therefore does not depend on our interests, beliefs, hopes, wishes, abilities, level of knowledge, and so on. This means also that moral truth "will be there" even without human existence and activities. To be clearer about this notion of realism in ethics, it is to say that moral truth is not contextual in any way and accordingly it is neither social nor political, nor cultural or historical.

On the other side, Anti-realism claims that moral truth is man-made and therefore it can be cultural or social. Such truth could even be created by an individual or an authority such as a social reformer, leader, or prophet. In the context of anti-realism, moral rightness and wrongness depends on human activities such as historical context and what people want to do, prefer, can do, or hope, and so on.

UNIVERSALISM VS. RELATIVISM IN ETHICS

Another important discussion in ethics is concerned with validity of moral laws or duties. The question: Are the standards of morality valid for all humans with different cultural backgrounds and different religious beliefs? Could we expect the same moral duty or obligation from everyone?

Universalists claim that standards of morality are unchanging and consequently they do not expire, nor are they limited to social, cultural, or historical circumstances. Everybody is familiar with universalists' claim that morality is not for sale and hence moral duties apply to everyone regardless of status, social and ethnic background, and so on. Accordingly certain "golden rules of morality" must be obeyed by all humans, and therefore lying, for example, is always wrong so is stealing and...(refer to the Ten Commandments).

On the other side, relativism defends the view that moral standards are subject to change and they depend on time and place, social and cultural views and interpretations, and so forth. Therefore lying is not always wrong since its rightness and wrongness depends on constantly changing factors and circumstances such as political views or scientific or some other dominating cultural worldview and belief. This view of relativism is also known as "live and let live," meaning that we should not convert people to moral understanding, and we must practice tolerance by accepting people as they are.

EPISTEMOLOGY OF ETHICS

One of the most relevant questions asked in ethics is how we know/how we are supposed to know about moral truth or moral imperatives, also known as moral commands. What is at stake is the reliability of moral knowledge or, even more important, the method that one has used for developing moral knowledge.

While in a religious framework, one can refer to a holy book or some spiritual/supernatural activity as the source of moral knowledge, in a critical context, the method and its reliability must be established first since the potential unreliability of the method can only lead to misjudgments and false beliefs.

REASONS FOR BEING MORAL

Another important question asked in ethics: why morality at all? In other words, even if we know about the standards of morality, why should we follow them, especially when they don't seem to be in our best interest? Again in a non-critical context, one can simply demand obedience or refer to God's will/ promises, potential rewards and punishments, to motivate individuals to care, but in a critical context, the ethicist is obligated *to explain why one should even consider morality as guiding criteria for living.*

As stated before, it is necessary that the ethicist explain why a person should sacrifice personal interests and beliefs just to honor moral values and commands.

DEONTOLOGICAL AND TELEOLOGICAL ETHICS

Another historically important classification in ethics is concerned with moral actions having intrinsic value or whether their value is determined instrumentally based on already achieved or potential end results of the action.

Teleological views are also known as consequentialist views, which presuppose that actions have instrumental value. This means that the outcome of a particular action justifies its moral rightness or wrongness. Accordingly, if the outcome is good, the action is moral, and in the case of a bad or undesirable outcome, the action is immoral.

Unlike teleological, deontological views, or categorical moral judgments, use and presuppose moral values intrinsically. For example, the good motive or good intention of the moral agent defines the moral value of an action intrinsically. Accordingly, actions are right or wrong in themselves, which means, for example, lying is wrong regardless of its outcome (how good or bad the outcome might be).

A NATURALISTIC INTRODUCTION TO PHILOSOPHY

Test your knowledge:

1) How is Ethics defined?

Morals, what is right and wrong

2) What is the difference between Ethics and Psychology?

Ethics is normative
psychology is descriptive

3) What does an Ethical Issue represent?

Something that questions a person's morality

4) What is the difference between Realism & Anti-realism in Ethics?

realism is moral truth that humans having control of it.

Antirealism says that moral truth is man made

5) Define Universalism & Relativism in Ethics.

Universalism says that morals last forever

6) Describe Deontological & Teleological Ethics.

7) What is the Purpose of Ethics?

8) What is the method used in Ethics?

Your Comments:

A NATURALISTIC INTRODUCTION TO PHILOSOPHY

SAMPLES OF MORAL THEORIES
CULTURAL RELATIVISM, KANTIAN ETHICS, UTILITARIANISM

CULTURAL RELATIVISM

Cultural Relativism is a form of relativism that is primarily a descriptive moral theory (descriptive moral theories describe the origin of moral beliefs). Accordingly, cultural relativism describes the origin of morality culturally.

This idea is preserved in the first premise of their argument:
P1: Morality is cultural
This premise states that morality is exclusively a cultural entity which means that moral values, beliefs, commands etc. are cultural in their nature and that any moral judgment about rightness and wrongness is a cultural judgment. This means that moral judgments always presuppose a cultural context even when it is not clearly stated.

What might be considered immoral in one culture, Is not in another.

The second premise states that cultures are fundamentally different:
P2: Cultures are different
With "fundamentally different," it is meant that the differences are not superficial, such as differences in language, rituals, and history ... but that the underlying values are different.

The third premise assumes that no culture is better than any other culture. Accordingly, while cultures are different, no culture is in a better position (no culture has a special status). P3 : No culture is better

In support of the third premise, cultural relativists explain that cultures cannot be compared, and, consequently, we cannot make any judgment regarding which culture is better, more advanced, less developed, etc. The reason why cultures cannot be compared is there are no non-cultural standards available that could allow a fair comparison.

To elaborate on this, one could say that any criteria used for comparing, for example, culture A with culture B would still be cultural and therefore biased (non-objective).

Challenging Cultural Relativism

The first premise can be challenged by stating that the assumption that morality is exclusively cultural has not been established by cultural relativists.
This is a very crucial assumption which simply asserts that, since cultures have their preferred moral views, no external (non-cultural) moral view is possible, but why?

What might be considered immoral in one culture, Is not in another.

Is this true?

In summary, although cultures could have their own particular interpretations or views about morality, this does not support the claim that moral truth is the creation of cultures.

The second premise, "cultures are different," can be challenged by stating that cultures are not as different as they appear. In fact, it seems that cultures share common beliefs, such as "do not kill," "do not steal," and so on. Further, all cultures MUST share certain values, because without them, no culture can exist.

Isn't it imaginable that, in addition to the cultural beliefs concerning rightness and wrongness, there could also be an objective (non-human) moral truth?
The point is that the presence of one does not need to exclude the other.

Cultural Beliefs

And

Moral Truth

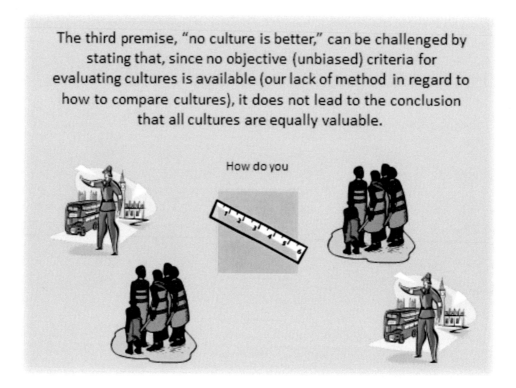

The third premise, "no culture is better," can be challenged by stating that, since no objective (unbiased) criteria for evaluating cultures is available (our lack of method in regard to how to compare cultures), it does not lead to the conclusion that all cultures are equally valuable.

How do you

STRENGTHS OF CULTURAL RELATIVISM

Cultural Relativism is a popular moral theory for two reasons: 1) because the theory is consistent with our experience of the world (other cultures), namely that cultures have their own moral understanding and beliefs, and 2) the theory promotes tolerance among cultures by stating that one culture is as valuable as any other.

PROBLEMS ASSOCIATED WITH CULTURAL RELATIVISM

There are also some weaknesses that are associated with cultural relativism, such as
tolerance that is valued by this theory becomes a problem. Accordingly, the theory is not capable of setting limits regarding what can be tolerated or not.

Further, cultural relativism can be understood as an attempt at building a new and superior culture that promotes tolerance while asserting that all cultures are equally valuable. But why should a culture of tolerance have a special place among all the other existing cultures?

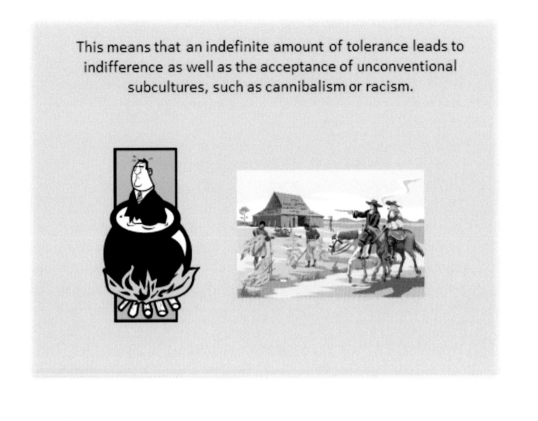

This means that an indefinite amount of tolerance leads to indifference as well as the acceptance of unconventional subcultures, such as cannibalism or racism.

Test your knowledge:

1. What is the argument in support of Cultural Relativism?

2. How can the assumptions (premises) that were used to develop the above argument be challenged?

3. What are the strengths and weaknesses of Cultural Relativism?

KANTIAN ETHICS

Kantian ethics is captured by the notion of Categorical Imperative. In fact, everything that Kant says is somehow linked to this notion. Generally speaking, Kant's Categorical Imperative is the moral law that one has to follow just by the virtue of being rational.

WHAT ARE THE DIFFERENCES BETWEEN
THE HYPOTHETICAL AND CATEGORICAL IMPERATIVES?

Kant introduces, explains, and validates his proposal (categorical imperative) in contrast to Hypothetical Imperative. While hypothetical is expressed in the form of a hypothetical or conditional statement (if you desire X, then do Y), the Categorical Imperative is expressed as an imperative that is right in itself, as is the case for all categorical moral judgments. In the case of categorical imperative, we are told to do Y for the sake of doing Y.

WHAT ARE KANTIAN DEFINITIONS OF CATEGORICAL IMPERATIVE?

Kant offers several definitions for Categorical Imperative. The first definition states: Act based on the principle that you can wish to be a universal law of nature (Universality). The second definition of categorical imperative states: Act based on the principle that treats rational beings as an end and never as a means to an end.

In the following, I aim to explain both definitions. They are two indispensable properties that Kant sees in his proposed moral law.

The first definition of Categorical Imperative is concerned with universality of a moral law. Accordingly, if a proposed moral law is not universal, it would mean that it is inconsistent and therefore irrational. This reasoning of Kant goes back to his understanding of reason and the overall project of Kant's philosophy, namely to introduce and promote enlightenment as a cultural movement. [2]

Taking into consideration that Categorical Imperative as a moral law is rational and therefore it is derived from reason, it must follow that it will be universal or unchanging. For example, lying is self-defeating or logically inconsistent, which presents the false statement as a true statement. Precisely due to this inconsistency (one claims to tell the truth, while this is not the case), lying is self-defeating and hence irrational and therefore not moral.

The second definition of Kant insists that it would be irrational to treat humans as means to an end. Specifically, the inconsistency of using humans as means to an end consists that moral law must be rational while humans themselves are rational beings (embodiment of moral law and reason). Therefore it would be self-defeating to treat a rational being irrationally.

STRENGTHS OF KANTIAN ETHICS

Kantian ethics is very systematic, rational, and well justified. In addition, Kant's moral system is based on Kantian metaphysics, which provides a solid foundation for his ethics. All in all, Kant's Categorical Imperative might be the most sophisticated and well-justified moral theory ever constructed, but in spite of its brilliance, there are some serious problems associated with it.

PROBLEMS ASSOCIATED WITH THE
FIRST DEFINITION OF CATEGORICAL IMPERATIVE

One problem associated with Kantian ethics is the potential conflicting Categorical Imperatives. Example: Telling the truth and saving a life. (Which has priority?) Kant does not consider the possibility of having conflicting and or competing categorical imperatives applicable to the same situation and therefore he does not offer a system or method for prioritizing one categorical imperative over another.

Another issue associated with Kant's moral philosophy is that Kantian ethics refuses to accept that the outcome of an action should be considered as well. There are many ways that the outcome or end result of an action could be calculated or be used as a factor for or during moral evaluations and considerations, but Kant leaves no room for that.

Above all, Kantian ethics is primarily concerned with the issue of a justified moral act based on the assumption that justification is the sole criteria for morality. The link or the guarantee that a rational choice must be a moral choice at the same time is simply assumed and not established by Kant.

Finally, one might say that Kantian ethics raises the standards of morality to the level that it becomes unrealistic for humans to meet Kantian expectations. Especially Kant's notion of "pure good will." This is unrealistic due to Kant's expectation that pure good will is entirely unselfish.

PUNISHMENT IN THE KANTIAN SYSTEM

Kant believes that we ought to punish criminals so that we can protect their dignity. Specifically, by holding the criminal accountable, we treat the criminal seriously as a rational being, which is the same as treating the criminal as he or she deserves to be treated, namely as an end.

Your Comments:

UTILITARIANISM

Utilitarianism is a theory that was originally invented by Jeremy Bentham (1748 – 1832). This theory was further developed by James Mill (1773 – 1836) and mostly by John Stuart Mill (1806 –1873).

From a utilitarian perspective, since the outcome of an action justifies its rightness (a priori assumption of the theory), and the most desirable outcome is the most amount of happiness (a priori assumption of the theory), it follows that actions are morally right if they create the most amount of happiness possible.

Further, since we all value democracy as an ideal system of governing and since utilitarianism offers an explanation for the legitimacy of this system, this should also establish the sophistication of utilitarianism not only as a moral theory but also as a social political theory.

PROBLEMS ASSOCIATED WITH THE THEORY

In spite of the commitment of this theory to happiness for most people, there are some serious issues associated with this theory. For one, the utilitarian notion of Justice, as it has to be defined consistent with the principle of utility, is in direct conflict with the commonsense understanding of Justice (Justice is served when it promotes happiness).

Another problem with utilitarianism is that as it claims to be realistic by describing how moral choices are already made, it becomes demanding/unrealistic by asserting that any moral choice has to create the greatest amount of happiness possible. The theory becomes unrealistic, for example, by demanding impartiality (happiness of our loved one should have the same amount of value as the happiness of a stranger) but also with demands such as one should sacrifice his/her own happiness for the happiness of the greatest number of people.

Test your knowledge:

1. What are the arguments in support of utilitarianism?

2. How can these arguments be challenged?

3. What is the difference between Act and Rule utilitarianism?

4. What is the utilitarian notion of happiness and why?

5. What is the utilitarian view about capital punishment, euthanasia, and animal rights?

6. What are the strengths and problems associated with utilitarianism?

Your Comments:

NATURALIZING ETHICS?

Should sciences contribute to ethics? If yes, how?

The relationship between ethics and science is complex, and it can be debated for a very long time, but the fact is sciences have produced and continue to produce factual knowledge of various kinds that are used indirectly in the area of applied ethics. Further, it would be naïve and pointless to ignore scientific knowledge and not include it in our daily moral considerations.

As far as the relationship between ethics and sciences, including medicine and psychology, is concerned, Sam Harris (2010) offers a naturalistic account in his published book, *Moral Landscape*. He proposes human well-being and human flourishing as guiding moral values; if certain actions should be judged as immoral. Harris points out that it can be determined "objectively" or scientifically which actions endanger human well-being and therefore are wrong such as honor killings in Pakistan and Jordan; the lashing of a fourteen-year-old girl to death for adultery in Bangladesh on March 28, 2011; and prearranged marriage of a thirteen-year-old girl with a sixty-five-year-old man in Afghanistan and Saudi Arabia.

Generally speaking, Harris rejects relativistic approaches in ethics and claims that by using science, one can determine which cultural activities are standing in the way of human well-being. In this context, he argues that although there is no "clear definition" of human well-being or "human health," this does not prevent psychologists, physicians, and other scientists from making their professional judgments on a daily basis concerning what is not "healthy" or what does not contribute to human well-being.

For more information concerning Harris's account and its potential, see "In Defense of Harris's Science of Morality" August/September 2013 issue of Free Inquiry Vol. 33 No. 5 [28–34].

Share your Comments:

Should sciences be used to establish physical harm and psychological injury caused by some cultural rituals such as female circumcision? Would you accept such scientific findings as evidence to condemn these rituals morally? Explain why.

Chapter 4
Epistemology

Epistemology is defined as the Study of Knowledge, also known as the theory of knowledge.

In Western epistemology, "knowing" is described as an "Intellectual process."
What makes knowing an intellectual process is that in Western epistemology, one knows or discovers "truth" by having a representation of ... (What defines knowledge as intellectual is that the essence of knowledge is representative).

A representation is a mental (cognitive) construct that is present as a state of awareness in the mind constituting knowledge.

The relationship between a representation and what a representation represents is often the center of epistemological studies, and it can be imagined in three possible ways:

1. A representation "corresponds" to the object represented. In this case, we have true belief or knowledge because representation is an accurate representation of what is "out there."

Example: Imagine that I have a Polaroid camera, which can take an instant picture. Let's assume that the picture that I take of you turns out good. In this case, the picture corresponds to your appearance because the picture resembles the way you are in reality (The picture represents you).

2. A representation does not correspond to the object represented. In this case, we have a false belief, which is NOT knowledge because the representation is a misrepresentation of the object represented.

Example: Assume that the Polaroid picture did not turn so well and you claim that the picture is unfair because you look much better in reality (picture misrepresents your appearance, hence does not correspond).

#%@*&I don't look that bad!!!!!

3. The third option is that a representation represents nothing (there is nothing out there that is being represented). Epistemologists often call such representations "pure representation."

Using the same example of the Polaroid camera, it would be like having a Polaroid picture of someone who never existed. As much as this option appears unrealistic, it is so that we sometimes dream (have a representation) of a place or an event or a person that we have not experienced before.

As stated already, what constitutes knowledge in western epistemology is the presence of a representation, but once there is a representation, it becomes necessary to ask how we establish the accuracy of this representation (how can it be demonstrated rationally that a representation is an accurate representation of object represented?)

Is that really me?

Further, Western epistemology has been historically concerned with questions such as "what is the most reliable method of gathering knowledge?" For example, should we use experience or should we use reason to develop knowledge? In this regard, we will see how empiricists and rationalists disagree over which type of knowledge is more dependable, (i.e., empirical knowledge or a priori knowledge).

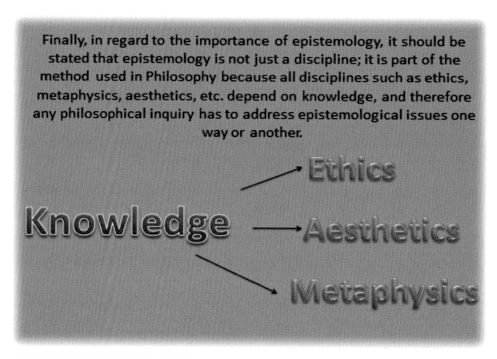

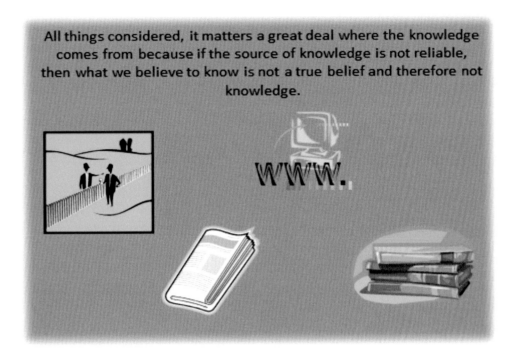

Test your knowledge:

1. Describe and discuss the importance of epistemology.

2. Explain what constitutes knowledge in Western epistemology and what issues are associated with it.

Note: It is important to stress that philosophy is not limited to Western philosophy and that there are major differences between Western and non-Western philosophies. The differences are also visible in epistemology when, for example, non-Western epistemologies define the nature of knowledge differently from how knowledge is defined in Western epistemology.

RATIONALISM

Rationalism is a theory of knowledge concerned with the source or origin of knowledge. According to rationalists, knowledge is based on reason, which means that the thinking process constitutes the a priori representation that makes knowledge possible. (A priori representations are representations that are not formed through experience).

Generally speaking, rationalists claim that a priori knowledge is dependable because empirical knowledge, or knowledge based on experience, is NOT. Specifically, the argument states that experience is unreliable because "experience" is deceiving. For example, how often have we been under the impression that we see or hear something, but after careful examination, we realize that it was just a mirage, an illusion, or perhaps a hallucination?

According to rationalists, "activities of reason" and **not** experience constitute knowing, "a priori knowledge."

Reason (activities of the mind that require judgments through *THINKING*) →constitute → a priori representation and with that, a priori knowledge

Either way, since we cannot be certain that what we experience is true, experience cannot be trusted as a source of knowledge.

Plato, one of the most influential philosophers in the western world, was a rationalist who believed that appearances given to us through experience are unreliable.

Other rationalists in the modern time were Spinoza, Leibniz, and Descartes.

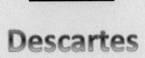

It is noteworthy that rationalists traditionally have been fascinated with mathematical sciences, and often they tried to "mathematize" philosophy.

Descartes, for example, who was a pioneer of modern analytic geometry, aimed to mathematize philosophy by developing an epistemology that resembles the method used by geometry for developing its knowledge.

During the period of scientific revolution, many rationalists, in particular Descartes, believed that scientific truth is captured through the "judgments of reason" and not through the appearances given to us by experience.

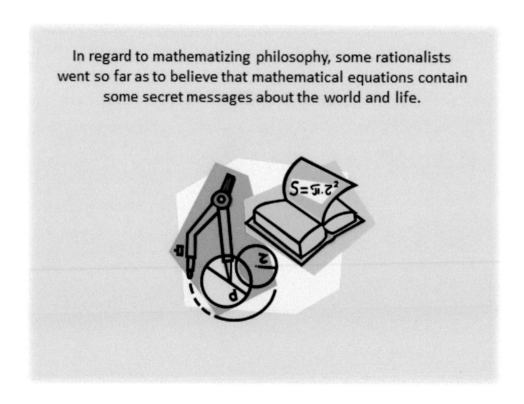

In regard to mathematizing philosophy, some rationalists went so far as to believe that mathematical equations contain some secret messages about the world and life.

In another example, Albert Einstein predicted the existence of a "black hole" in the center of our galaxy many years before astronomers could confirm its existence. (A black hole is an extremely dense star with such enormous gravity that not even light can escape from its gravitational field.)

Further, rationalists argue that magicians with their simple tricks confirm the overall claim of rationalism that experience cannot be trusted.

Finally, rationalists argue that the representations of time and space are not given to us through experience (we do not see, smell, touch, hear, or taste time or space). Accordingly, we have a representation of time as the result of our JUDGMENT about experiencing changes in our world.

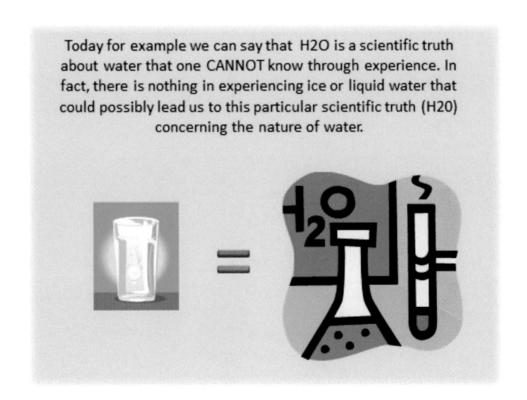

Today for example we can say that H2O is a scientific truth about water that one CANNOT know through experience. In fact, there is nothing in experiencing ice or liquid water that could possibly lead us to this particular scientific truth (H20) concerning the nature of water.

The point is that Einstein discovered the existence of black holes using mathematical equations without using direct observation through a telescope, in other words, without any experience.

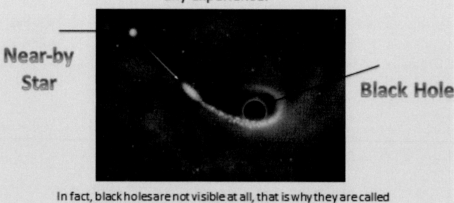

In fact, black holes are not visible at all, that is why they are called black holes.
We can only intimate they are there by viewing what they do to nearby stars.

Similarly, we have *a priori* representations of space, not because we can see, hear, touch, smell, or taste space, but because we have a non-empirical representation of space formed through a JUDGMENT, such as objects can only exist IN space.

Test your knowledge:

1. What is the main argument in support of rationalism?

2. Who are the main modern rationalists?

3. Explain why time is an a priori representation and not an empirical representation.

Your Comments:

RATIONALISM OF DESCARTES

PART 1

CARTESIAN ARGUMENT IN SUPPORT OF RATIONALISM

Descartes's argument in support of rationalism aims at discrediting experience as a reliable source of knowledge.

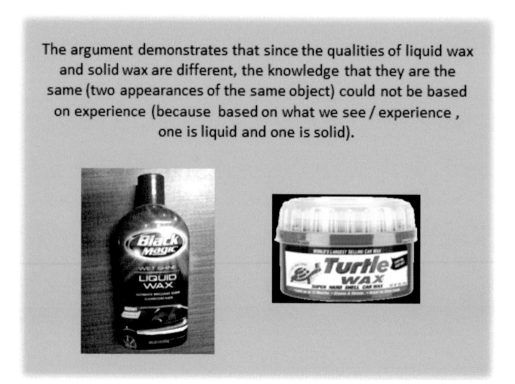

The argument demonstrates that since the qualities of liquid wax and solid wax are different, the knowledge that they are the same (two appearances of the same object) could not be based on experience (because based on what we see / experience, one is liquid and one is solid).

The main point of this argument is to state that we know more than what we can experience, and consequently, the <u>judgment that both objects (liquid wax and solid wax) are different appearances of the same object</u> could not have had its source in experience but rather in thinking (reason).

In this regard, Descartes aims to establish that it is the <u>interpretation of experience</u> and not just "experience" such as seeing, smelling, or touching that leads to our knowledge of the world.

Objective of Cartesian Epistemology:

The foundation of Cartesian epistemology is laid out in the first Meditation*.

*http://www.wright.edu/cola/descartes/mede.html or
http://oregonstate.edu/instruct/phl302/texts/descartes/meditations/meditations.html

In particular, Descartes aims to clarify the problem of skepticism concerning our experience of the world. Radical Skeptics claim that Knowledge is not possible because all knowledge remains uncertain, and by "uncertainty," it is meant that **no** knowledge is definite as well as **no** knowledge can be justified.

Descartes' systematic Doubt:

Descartes' systematic doubt can be understood as a strategy of Descartes to overcome skepticism (to change the uncertainty to certainty) by beginning with skepticism.

Uncertainty

Skepticism

Certainty

In accordance with this method, there are three grounds for doubt: Hallucinations, Dreams and Illusions.

HALLUCINATIONS

It is notable that Descartes accepts the skeptics' view, namely that no knowledge is certain, only to find a way out of skepticism.

Further, he hopes that by using this method, he can avoid mistakes such as assuming something that is not true.

Skeptics View

Hallucinations: Our experience of the world could be mere hallucination.

Skeptics challenge the notion that we are experiencing a world.

Accordingly, the world could be the product of our own mind (people with schizophrenia cannot tell the difference between what is real and what is not).

Descartes presents the following question: How do we know that we are not experiencing our own hallucination while we believe that we are experiencing an "objective" reality.

REAL OR NOT REAL?

Dreams: Our experience of the world could be a dream which means that at this moment we could be dreaming that we are discussing Philosophy while in "reality" we are actually sleeping.

Descartes argues that while we are dreaming we are not aware that the experience is not real so the dream world presents itself to us often as vivid as the experience we have right now.

Illusions: Our experience of reality could be an illusion (see the movie *The Matrix*). Just as *The Matrix* is a computer-generated virtual reality, it is possible that our experience of the world is a virtual experience, and, consequently, what we consider as real is nothing but an appearance and therefore does not exist independently from us.

Origin of Cogito Statement

All things considered, Descartes concludes that our experience of the world could be illusion, dream or hallucination; therefore, their existence can be doubted.

Illusion

Dream

Hallucination

Further, Descartes argues that everything should be and can be the subject of doubt, but there is one thing that cannot be doubted, and that is "doubting." This means that the actual thinking process of "doubting" cannot be doubted or questioned, because if we choose to doubt "doubting," then it would be that we must presuppose the existence of doubting while we aim at challenging it; therefore, Descartes concludes that doubting must exist, but what is the nature of doubting?

Descartes responds by saying that "doubting" is a mind activity ** and specifically a form of thinking, and since doubting cannot be doubted (see previous slide), we must conclude that a thinking mind, which is required to have doubts, must exist.

In addition, Descartes states that if I am the person who thinks by doubting, then it follows that I must exist (my doubt proves my existence) / "Cogito ergo sum," or, I think, therefore I am.

**It is noteworthy that Descartes was the first philosopher who defined the mind as psychology defines it today, namely as a thinking thing, experiencing, affirming, denying, desiring,...thing. It must also be added that Descartes' proposal of this notion of mind was a replacement for the soul as Greek philosophy traditionally was obsessed with.

Test your knowledge:

1) What is the purpose of Cartesian epistemology?

2) What is the Cartesian method for achieving the above goal?

3) Describe and discuss the origin of the Cogito statement.

Your Comments:

Rationalism of Descartes
PART 2

The purpose of Cartesian epistemology was to develop a "new philosophy" (a new system of thinking for philosophizing as such).

The idea was that this new system of thought should be able to achieve the certainty of knowledge and to withstand the tests and challenges of skepticism.

Descartes, who was himself one of the founding fathers of modern analytic Geometry, was convinced that geometry provided an ideal model for developing a new system of thinking.

Some of his ideas are captured in the following:

•Authorities should have no place in a philosophical inquiry as they have no place in geometry.

•Philosophical issues should be discussed as carefully and systematically as issues are discussed and proven in geometry.

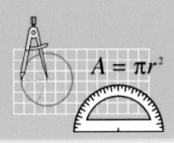

$$A = \pi r^2$$

•Deductive reasoning should be the preferred method of reasoning, as it is in geometry.

•Any deductive system such as Geometry is based on self-evident axioms; therefore, a similar foundation is required for the "new system of thinking in Philosophy." In fact, Descartes's cogito statement (I think, therefore I am) is supposed to be the self-evident axiom needed to construct a new, deductive Philosophy similar to geometry.

I  Therefore

Descartes' argument in support of God:

Descartes developed several arguments in support of God, but perhaps the most important deductive argument is known as the ontological argument.

P1: God is defined as a perfect being

P2: Nothing is perfect unless it exists

C: God exists

What Descartes aims to deduce with this argument is that by definition, the notion of a perfect being contains an existential claim. Accordingly, "perfect being" as an a priori representation is an exception among a priori representations because it is the only representation of this type with the claim that the object represented (God) must exist.

Mission of Cartesian Project:

The mission of the Cartesian project is to develop a reliable method for answering metaphysical questions.
In short, the Cartesian attempt to develop a more sophisticated epistemology aims at becoming the necessary means for answering questions concerning the experienced reality.

Descartes aims to establish the existence of God because he then uses the existence and perfection of God to prove the existence of a material world.

God is Perfect

Therefore

Specifically, the argument states that God is no deceiver (God is too perfect to deceive), and therefore the material world that we experience is neither an illusion nor a hallucination and therefore real.

God is no Deceiver

Is Real

A NATURALISTIC INTRODUCTION TO PHILOSOPHY

Test your knowledge:

1) What is the purpose of the Cogito Statement?

2) What is Descartes's argument that the material world exists?

Your Comments:

EMPIRICISM

Introduction to Empiricism

The modern empiricists John Locke, George Berkeley, and David Hume believed that representations or ideas are either formed directly through sense-experience or they have their origins in experience.

For example, there is no memory in the mind (memories count as ideas or representations) that is not linked to an experience in the past. In this regard, empiricists were interested in explaining the origin of all representations in general and empirical representations in particular.

It is important to emphasize this aspect, namely that empiricists have a very limited and specific understanding of what counts as "experience." In short, with "experience" empiricists have neither "spiritual experience" in mind nor general ideas like "My vacation was a wonderful experience." When empiricists refer to experience as the source of knowledge, they mean sense-experience, such as seeing, hearing, smelling, touching, and tasting.

For example, how could we know about Chinese food unless we taste it (just by thinking hard, we will never know its taste).

Example: Imagine that one is born with no ability to experience, which means that one cannot see, hear, touch, taste, or smell. Is there anything about the world that this person can know? Most likely not, empiricists respond.

Arguments in support of Empiricism

The main argument in support of empiricism states that when it comes to developing factual knowledge (knowledge about the world), there is no alternative to experience.

Experience → Knowledge

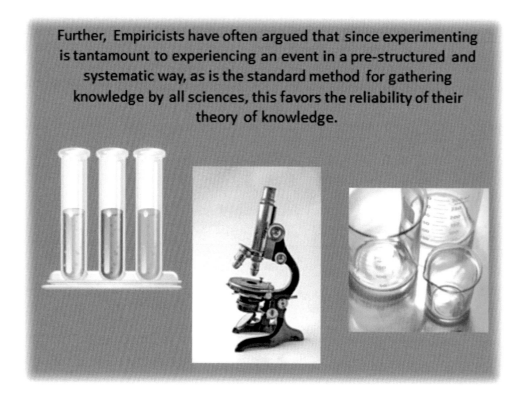

Further, Empiricists have often argued that since experimenting is tantamount to experiencing an event in a pre-structured and systematic way, as is the standard method for gathering knowledge by all sciences, this favors the reliability of their theory of knowledge.

In other words, since physics, chemistry, biology, medicine, and other natural sciences use empiricists' method of knowledge—namely systematic observation, called experiment—to capture the "truth" in their respective disciplines, experience must be a reliable source of knowledge.

ADDITIONAL COMMENTS ABOUT EMPIRICISM

Since empiricists explain the origin of knowledge passively by saying that the observer is not actively involved in knowledge formation (ideas are formed through sense-experience with very little or almost no thinking process), the philosophy of the mind that empiricists presuppose for their theory of knowledge is not as complex as the rationalists'.

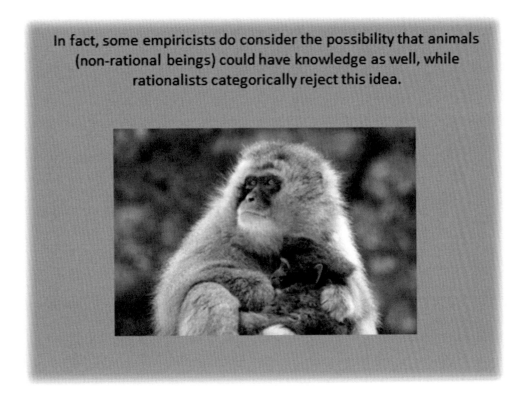

In fact, some empiricists do consider the possibility that animals (non-rational beings) could have knowledge as well, while rationalists categorically reject this idea.

Rationalists often argued that since the ability to understand constitutes knowing, since animals are unable to "understand" their experience, only humans as rational beings are privileged to have KNOWLEDGE. In addition, the empiricist's theories of knowledge are often aimed at describing and explaining the origin of common sense or daily knowledge as much as the origin of scientific and philosophical knowledge.

In some cases, empiricists intended to describe how daily knowledge takes part in the formation of scientific and philosophical knowledge (how daily knowledge is linked to the process by which scientific knowledge and philosophical knowledge are formed). Contrary to empiricists, rationalists had the tendency to stay "above the clouds" by excluding/avoiding daily knowledge or commonsense knowledge in their explanations.

Test your knowledge:

1. What is the empiricists' notion of experience?

2. Who are the main modern empiricists?

3. What are the arguments in support of empiricism?

4. Explain why empiricists presuppose a simpler theory of mind than rationalists do?

Non-Western Epistemology

In addition to representative types of knowledge, many non-Western epistemologies refer to another type of knowledge which is not intellectual but emotional and experiential, called "intuitive knowledge"

Intuitive Knowledge is often dismissed by Western epistemologists as "knowledge" and rather categorized as opinion / belief.

It is noteworthy that non-Western epistemologies are also concerned with intellectual or representative knowledge, but in contrast to Western epistemology, they often emphasize intuitive knowledge over intellectual knowledge.

Here are some examples of non-representative / intuitive knowledge:

Indian Philosophy: *Darsana*

Japanese Philosophy: *Satori*

Native American Philosophy: Knowledge by *hanblechia*

It is crucial to underline that although intuitive knowledge is not intellectual in its nature, some Philosophers have demonstrated that intuitive knowledge can be discussed intellectually.

Example: I can have an awareness of a physical pain which is a feeling, but I can also describe my pain (this particular feeling) to someone through language and thereby construct a representation of pain. In this regard, the representation of pain is not a requirement (condition for knowing) that "I am in pain."

Representative Knowledge: 1. Representation   constitutes→ 2. Knowing

Intuitive Knowledge: Knowing intuitively (awareness or knowing as we are experiencing...)

SOME CHARACTERISTICS OF NON-WESTERN EPISTEMOLOGIES

Asian Epistemology:

Asian epistemology emphasizes Intuitive knowledge, which is emotional, personal, and experiential. In accordance with Asian epistemology, one *realizes* the truth through purification of the spirit and detachment from the material world. This means that the spirit must be "prepared" for detecting the truth, and detachment from the material world, including "meditations," is part of this process of getting the human spirit / soul "ready."

SOME CHARACTERISTICS OF NON-WESTERN EPISTEMOLOGIES

African Epistemology:

African epistemology shares both Western and Asian epistemic views. Accordingly, there is knowledge that is intellectual and there is knowledge that is intuitive. What separates African epistemology from Western and Asian theories of knowledge is that Community collectively _experiences_ the truth and _tells_ the truth. In short, it is not the philosopher or the wise man who discovers / constructs the truth but rather the entire community that participates in this process.

SOME CHARACTERISTICS OF NON-WESTERN EPISTEMOLOGIES

Native American Epistemology:

Similar to Asian epistemology, Native American theories of knowledge emphasize the nature of knowledge as being intuitive. Accordingly, one _realizes_ the truth through visions and dreams. Although Native American epistemology believes that knowledge can be transferred from one person to another person through stories ..., the ultimate truth about "self" and the world is known subjectively by experiencing the truth first hand.

Due to the exclusive emphasis of Native American epistemology on intuitive knowledge (non-representative knowledge) over than intellectual (representative) knowledge, epistemic truth of native American Philosophies can neither be demonstrated through ordinary language nor can it be supported or established using traditional methods of justification (Argument).

Test your knowledge:

1. What is the main difference between African epistemology and other types of epistemologies?

2. What is the main difference between Western epistemology and non-Western epistemologies?

Your Comments:

HUME'S EMPIRICISM

David Hume is certainly one of the most important thinkers, empiricists, and philosophers of all time. Consistent with the empiricist tradition, Hume distinguishes between impressions and ideas while he considers "Impressions" as the source of ideas.

RELATIONS OF IDEAS (A PRIORI KNOWLEDGE)

Hume distinguishes between two types of knowledge. One is a priori knowledge, which he calls relations of ideas, and the other one is empirical knowledge, which he calls knowledge of Matters of Fact.

Hume explains the relations of ideas by stating that since this type of knowledge is not based on experience, the subject of knowledge does not exist (only things that exist can be experienced). Further, the truth of this type of knowledge, such as mathematical knowledge and formula logic is demonstrable, meaning it can be justified.

For example, a triangle, the number 7, and hypothetical syllogisms do not actually exist in the real world (as physical objects or entities); our knowledge about them is certain, such as the sum of the angles of any triangle is 180, 3+4 = 7, and hypothetical syllogisms are valid deductive arguments.

KNOWLEDGE OF MATTERS OF FACT (EMPIRICAL KNOWLEDGE)

This type of knowledge is the main focus of Hume's epistemological studies. Hume clarifies characteristics of this form of knowledge by stating that since empirical knowledge is gathered through experience, the subject of this type of knowledge exists. For the sake of clarity, it needs to be stated that with knowledge of Matters of Fact, Hume means factual knowledge about things that exist (one cannot experience something that it is not there). Further, since the truth of this knowledge is known only through experience, logic or reason cannot provide any proof or certainty of its truth, such as fire is hot, grass is green, and so on.

Finally, Hume demonstrates that all knowledge of Matters of Fact represents causal relationships, meaning causality is the condition under which any empirical knowledge is developed. It is noteworthy concerning Hume's understanding of Matters of Facts that ANY knowledge we gather based on experience, including daily knowledge as well as knowledge that is developed in natural sciences (such as physics, chemistry, biology, astronomy, etc.), also communicates causal relationships.

All things considered, knowledge of Matters of Fact relies on experience and it "communicates" a causal link between an event and the following event, which could also include the relationship that apparently exists between an object and its particular quality such as ice is cold, fire is hot, grass is green.

INTENTION OF HUMEAN EPISTEMOLOGY

The intention of Humean epistemology was to justify empiricism. Justifying empiricism means that Hume aimed at demonstrating (rationally using arguments) that knowledge based on experience is dependable-/unchanging and therefore experience as the source of knowledge can be trusted. Unlike rationalism (claiming that experience is not reliable), Hume as a devoted empiricist, was entirely focused on establishing that all of our knowledge comes from experience. Further, it became part of his epistemological project to demonstrate the dependability or certainty of such knowledge.

All things considered, Hume identified causality as the key assumption used for knowledge of Matters of Fact. On this background, Hume concluded that justifying empirical knowledge requires a justified account of causality. In other words, since causality is the underlying principle presupposed for any knowledge that is developed through experience, Hume demanded a justification or proof for the Principle of Causality. Humean demand for a justified account of causality is to be understood as an attempt to seek an argument that establishes the certainty of any causal relationship such as the following:

1) How do we know that the same cause creates the same effect?

2) How do we know that a causal relationship between two phenomena is valid everywhere?

3) How do we know that causality between two phenomena will also exist in the future?

In summary, Hume is seeking an argument in defense of the claim that there is a necessary connection between two events that are causally linked.

OUTCOME OF HUME'S INQUIRY ABOUT THE CERTAINTY-/VALIDITY OF EMPIRICAL KNOWLEDGE

Hume admitted in spite of his careful analytical studies and research that he was unable to find any argument that could justify causal relationships, and due to absence of such an argument, he concluded that the empirical knowledge (knowledge of Matters of Fact) remains uncertain or unjustified, and therefore skepticism becomes inescapable.

HUMEAN EXPLANATION ABOUT THE ORIGIN OF CAUSALITY

Although Hume was unable to justify empiricism as originally intended, he offered an explanation concerning how one knows that A and B are in a causal relationship. In this regard, Hume argued that since the act of "thinking," or one might say "reason," cannot demonstrate "the necessity" associated with causal relationships, it must follow that causality has psychological origin, meaning also that a psychological process is responsible for its formation.

Hume states clearly that causality is a creation of mind. Accordingly, the source of such creation is custom or habit (by a constant conjunction of event A and event B, we come to anticipate B whenever we experience A). In other words, Hume used the association of two ideas to explain the origin of causal relationships.

Test your knowledge:

1) What is the origin of ideas according to Hume?

2) What is "relations of ideas" according to Hume?

3) What is "Matters of Fact" according to Hume?

4) What was the intention of Humean epistemology?

5) What are the Humean questions?

6) What is the outcome of Humean epistemology and why?

7) What is the origin of any causal relationship according to Hume?

Your Comments:

NATURALIZED EPISTEMOLOGY

As already explained in the first chapter, naturalized epistemology is an attempt to integrate epistemology into science or science into epistemology. With these integrations, this means that any naturalized account would have to seek a transition from normative judgments to descriptive judgments while replacing a priori knowledge with empirical knowledge. The history of the relationship between philosophy and science shows that transitions of this kind (normative to descriptive) have been patterns and are by no means exceptional. Cosmology, Psychology and Anthropology for example are normative disciplines while they are operating currently in descriptive frameworks.

The task of naturalized epistemology is to accelerate this existing historical "trend" concerning the relationship between philosophy and science. Accordingly, it will be the final objective of naturalized epistemology to make the transition from the normative to a descriptive and empirical epistemology under the umbrella of cognitive psychology.

WHY ONE OUGHT TO SEEK NATURALIZED EPISTEMOLOGY?

There are several reasons that could be merged in to one; namely, naturalizing epistemology would be mutually beneficial to epistemology and psychology both.

1) It helps epistemology "mature" into science by which its further development will be greatly enhanced.

2) It helps psychology to develop new theoretical tools and concepts concerning the activities of the human mind through which psychology gets closer to its vision of becoming a science of human psyche.

Let's take one step back and ask ourselves about the mission of epistemology today. Is there a grand project that epistemology (as a whole) is pursuing or is supposed to pursue? Looking at the history of Western epistemology, there are some classic objectives such as overcoming skepticism, which I, personally, doubt to be achievable in a Cartesian sense.

Again, what is the final goal or purpose of western epistemology? Although there are many objectives to be pursued in epistemology, it also appears that epistemology has become the study of collecting as many theories of knowledge and concepts of various kinds as possible, but is this dilemma facing the current state of epistemology? Do epistemologists become conceptual hoarders simply collecting various accounts of knowledge without any specific project insight that could organize, direct, and bundle all the existing efforts and theories in to one particular objective?

In contrast to the traditional normative epistemology, the objective of naturalized epistemology can be stated more clearly. The objective would be to "bundle" all efforts into one goal, namely laying down the groundwork for epistemology maturing into an independent science. This objective is a long-term objective, and it cannot be completed by epistemologists alone. Not to mention that today's epistemologists will not live long enough to witness the transition of epistemology in to an independent science. Nevertheless, today's epistemologists could lay the theoretical foundation for this process to begin and to accelerate.

Should this goal be reached at some point in the future, epistemology like any other science will develop its own method and procedure for examining its issues, including the origin of knowledge as well as the procedure for its validation. As already mentioned, transitions of this kind have happened before in the history of philosophy in disciplines such as anthropology, psychology, and cosmology.

A brief historical survey of these disciplines shows that as normative disciplines have evolved, they became more sophisticated by forming an internal structure, system, and methodology for examining the problems that are embedded in their disciplinary interests.

HOW DO WE BEGIN THE PROJECT?

Although it would be counterintuitive to prescribe how the transition from normative to descriptive should be achieved, most likely there would be at least two phases for this transition.

1) *The Pre-scientific Phase,* which is about jump-starting science. This phase not only includes replacing a priori concepts with empirically based concepts, but it also is about reformulating questions while avoiding traditional metaphysical terms such as "being," "nature," or "essence" of things. Accordingly, the following questions are no longer permissible:

   A) What is the nature of knowledge?
   B) What constitutes moral truth?
   C) What is the essence of reality?

2) *The Scientific Phase,* which is based on the previous phase, continues with minimizing and ideally eliminating all a priori concepts. Further, this phase is about actively applying the scientific approach, knowledge, and other procedures.

The difference between these two steps is that while the first phase prepares the analytic framework required for naturalizing epistemology, the second phase actively applies empirically based descriptions concerning the origin of knowledge.

To illustrate this envisioned epistemological project to be completed in the second phase, it is to say that naturalized epistemology seeks scientific explanations regarding how any knowledge is possible by offering a detailed demonstration of all activities of the mind through which the presence of a state of knowing in the consciousness can be accounted for psychologically.

Chapter 5
Metaphysics

Introduction to Metaphysics

Metaphysics is known as the study of reality.
With the word "real," metaphysicians understand principles
or concepts that are basic or fundamental.

Basic principles of physics

Basic principles of genetics

Basic principles of political philosophy

These principles are fundamental because they are not only independent (exist independently) , but also because they provide a foundation for explanations.

Why planets appear to make loops in the their orbits

Explain Why

Kepler's Third Law

In short, metaphysical theories are there to explain the origin of what is not real (illusion or appearance) based on what is real.

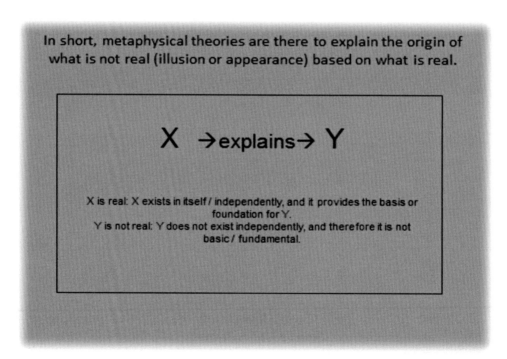

X →explains→ Y

X is real: X exists in itself / independently, and it provides the basis or foundation for Y.
Y is not real: Y does not exist independently, and therefore it is not basic / fundamental.

The fact that metaphysical theories are explanatory has created new issues, such as whom should we trust when it comes to explanations, or who can explain things better: scientists or philosophers?

Many contemporary philosophers prefer scientific explanations over philosophical explanations, and the differences are obvious. While scientific explanations are descriptive and empirical, philosophical explanations are normative (prescriptive) and a priori.

Scientist: I 'm right. There's evidence for the Big Bang.

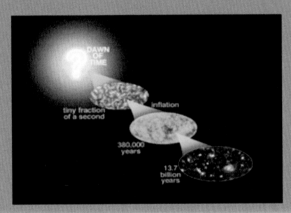

There are three types of metaphysical theories:

Idealism

Materialism

DUALISM

Idealism states that ideas with their immaterial nature are **real** (more fundamental), and physical objects with their material nature are **appearances** ("Mind over Matter").

Materialism is the metaphysical view stating that the material-/physical world is real, and ideas are illusions. In this case we have "matter over mind."

Materialists are **realists** (realists believe that the material world, which is distinct from the mind, exists independently from human thoughts and experience in general). In fact, materialists preferably refer to scientific views and explanations to support their claim that bio-chemical activities of the human brain are responsible (as the cause) for mind activities.

Such claims can be confirmed based on the following common knowledge; namely, individuals under the influence of drugs behave differently from when they are sober. In this case, activities of the brain control these changes, which would be consistent with the claim that activities that are material have priority over activities that are not material (matter is more basic and fundamental than the mind).

It is notable that with "matter," materialists see things that can be described in time-space, or, in general, entities that are tangible and can be experienced by our senses. Or they see things that can be measured scientifically.

NAÏVE REALISM

Physical or material objects exist the way they appear. These objects have physical characteristics such as color, sound, odor, shape, size, texture, and so forth.

These qualities are essential parts of what these objects are and therefore characteristics of the external world. From the view of naïve realism or direct realism, there is not much left to be explained metaphysically, since we are able to experience the world as it exists in itself. Direct realism claims that we are passive observers and hence, the experienced world is identical with the world that is "out there" distinct from the mind.

SCIENTIFIC REALISM

Scientific realism as a form of materialism presupposes that physical or material objects exist independently from our existence and our experience of them, but these objects do not "exist" the way they appear. Further, scientific realism aims at explaining the origin of these qualities that objects appear to have scientifically, such as color and sound. Consider sound for instance: We are told that sound consists of vibration of air molecules. Accordingly, once the vibration is detected by the eardrum, or tympanic membrane, electric signals are sent to the brain and the sound is created "in the brain." The bottom line is that vibration is not sound yet, although it is needed as a condition for creating sound.

Another example would be the origin of color that is explained scientifically using physics, chemistry, biology, medicine, and neurosciences. Accordingly, the amount of energy that is reflected from an object by so-called subatomic particles, known also as photons, is detected by human eyes and sent through the nervous system to the brain. Only then, after "the interpretation of this energy" is processed by the brain, will objects appear in color. If the particles carry a low level of energy/frequency, objects will appear reddish, and if the particles carry a high level of energy or frequency, they will appear bluish or greenish.

The point is that objects have no color and, in general, there is no "color" in the world, although we experience the world in a colorful way. Having said that, there is some property in each object that is responsible for how the energy is "translated" by the brain as a particular color.

In other words, scientific realism presupposes an external physical world or reality with its own independent features while it takes advantage of scientific knowledge to explain why this independent physical world appears the way it does. This account of reality is important for the project of this book, namely discussing a naturalistic account of the experienced world. (For more on this topic see the last chapter of this book concerning a psychological theory of experience.)

CHALLENGING SCIENTIFIC REALISM (SCIENTIFIC INSTRUMENTALISM)

Scientific Instrumentalism questions the validity of scientific explanations provided by Scientific Realists. Such a challenge is based on the argument that Scientific Realists misunderstand the nature of scientific knowledge and the abilities of sciences in general.

Instrumentalism is the philosophy of science defended by pragmatism. Pragmatists argue, using pragmatist truth concepts, that epistemic truth, or true knowledge, is nothing but an instrument or tool that is designed to serve a purpose/satisfy certain interests and therefore it will be replaced at some point by other tools (other true beliefs) that can serve the same interests or purpose more effectively. In other words, scientific instrumentalism challenges the view of scientific realism that theoretical entities like photons, electrons, and other so-called subatomic particles actually exist in the real world.

From the perspective of instrumentalism, photons are theoretical constructs of physics only, and they serve a specific purpose such as explaining how colors originate. Nevertheless, these particles do not exist as things in the world, as future science will use some other theoretical entities to explain the human experience of color.

All things considered, instrumentalism claims that the metaphysical explanation of scientific realism is not correct due to the false assumption of realism concerning the existence of these particles in reality. These particles, pragmatists argue, are only useful temporary assumptions or tools that scientists have applied until better (more functional) theoretical constructs are developed.

EXAMPLES FOR REALISM VS. ANTI-REALISM IN SCIENCE

REALISM: NEWTONIAN PHYSICS

Metaphysical Assumptions of Newton: A priori assumptions of Newton

  a) Realism: World exists independently from the observer
  b) Time is absolute
  c) An object can exist in only one location at a particular time
  d) Determinism

All of the above assumptions are consistent with our experience of the world. Because of this consistency, Newtonian physics is "understandable." Newtonian physics offered predictability and an "understanding of the world."

ANTI-REALISM: QUANTUM PHYSICS

Metaphysical Assumptions of Quantum theory: A priori assumptions of Quantum theory

  a) Anti-realism: reality depends on the observer (choices of the observer and his interests)
  b) Time is not absolute
  c) Subatomic particles can be in two places at the same time
  d) In-determinism

Quantum Physics offers only predictability and control but not an "understanding of the world." The reason for lack of understanding is that the assumptions of Quantum Physics are not consistent with our experience of the world.

Realism in Science

Scientific truth is discovered

Claim:

Structure of the scientific theory ———corresponds to the structure of reality———> Structure of the experienced Reality

(Correspondence truth concept)

Explanation:

Dependability of science can be explained because the representation of reality captured by the scientific truth "correctly" represents the reality as it exist independently from the mind.

Example: Considering the fact that huge numbers of airplanes take off and land safely world wide, this suggests that reality is accurately understood and represented by the science of aerodynamics.

Argument:

The uniqueness of scientific truth and its mathematical expression establishes the claim that only a correct representation of reality could explain the success of science (Not any arbitrary mathematical expression could make science work).
Example: $E=mc2$ works but not $E=m.c/2$ or $E=m.cx12$ or .....

Anti-realism in Science

Scientific truth is constructed

Claim:

Scientific truth / entity is only an instrument or tool. It is true because it works.

(Pragmatic truth concept)

Explanation:

There is always a guiding interest that shapes the research and its outcome (scientific truth). There is no scientific truth that is not designed to achieve certain human objectives (satisfy particular human interests).

Argument:

The history of science shows that scientific theories are replaced. There is no unchanging / irreplaceable truth in science, and this suggests that any truth in science is temporary and therefore only a tool until the next research constructs a more useful instrument that replaces the old one.

Your Comments:

125

DUALISM

Dualism is another metaphysical theory asserting that material and immaterial entities are both real, therefore, Dualism is unable to explain the origin of either of these two entities. In short, since dualists are not monoists (like idealists and materialists), they do not aim to explain one entity based on another. But Dualism still faces the problem of explaining how mind and body can communicate and/or why there is any interaction between mind and body at all.

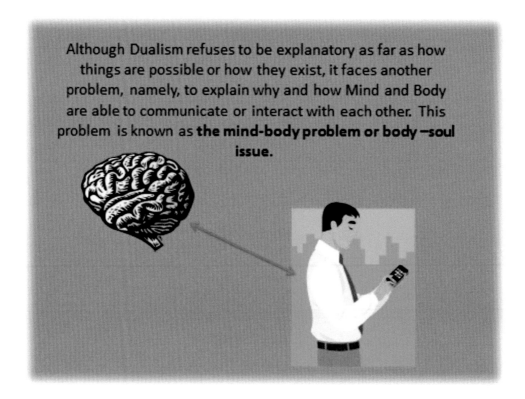

Although Dualism refuses to be explanatory as far as how things are possible or how they exist, it faces another problem, namely, to explain why and how Mind and Body are able to communicate or interact with each other. This problem is known as **the mind-body problem or body –soul issue.**

The center of the problem is that such interactions should not be possible at all. To elaborate on this issue, I will introduce the following example: Imagine that you are on the phone talking with someone in Japan. You speak only English and the other person speaks Japanese only. As we know, English and Japanese have nothing in common (these are two fundamentally different languages). Given these circumstances, is it possible for you to have a meaningful conversation with that individual?

The answer is obviously NO. Now, if mind and body are two distinct entities like the example used above (different because matter is "physical" but mind and its activities are not), then how and why are they able to communicate? Such interaction should not be possible (**wishing** to move your **physical arm** in a desired direction leads to the ability to do so).

Test your knowledge:

1. What is the function of a metaphysical theory?

2. Why is traditional metaphysics in a struggle?

3. What is meant by **realism** in metaphysics?

4. What is Idealism?

5. What is Materialism?

6. What is Naïve Realism?

7. What is Scientific Realism?

8. What is Scientific Instrumentalism?

9. What is Dualism?

Your Comments:

Chapter 6
Metaphilosophy of Naturalism

As it was explained in the first chapter, philosophy is "critical" and defining philosophy as a critical activity not only has profound implications of how philosophy should be practiced, but also of how it should be taught. Unlike some popular views, teaching philosophy is not a story telling activity that introduces the "profound ideas" of a few "great minds." For example, teaching allegory of the cave requires the critical examination of the language of Plato, including his key notions, concepts and beliefs, as well as the method he adopted for his introduction of ontological dualism. The point is that just sharing this story with students does not translate into "teaching philosophy". Teaching philosophy has to be significantly more than a simple reconstruction of a story that we admire as a culture and enthusiastically and repeatedly tell ourselves. In short, there have to be certain features or characteristics that are exclusive to activities that we refer to as philosophical; otherwise, there would be no difference between a philosophical work and other literary works, such as poetry.

Having said that, it is very difficult to set clear boundaries as far as what makes an idea or work philosophical, but having blurred lines and gray areas still allows for the discussion and evaluation of philosophical works, and is better than having no boundaries at all.

So what is it that makes an activity philosophical? The shortest answer would be that *philosophy is critical to the degree that other disciplines and other literally works are not.* What is meant by "more critical" in this context is that philosophizing as an intellectual activity is not limited to identifying, understanding and interpreting what has been said, or even interpreting an idea from different points of view, but rather *to be inquisitive and skeptical about what has been said by challenging the validity or legitimacy of the idea itself.* Furthermore, any critical activity presupposes a high degree of analysis, such as identifying all the components of a concept and its key assumptions so they can be challenged critically, including the context in which they are presented.

In summary, without analysis and intense critical inquiries as described above, there would be no difference between philosophy and the humanities, or philosophy and history. In the absence of these characteristics, philosophy could easily be mistaken as pseudo-anthropology or literary analysis especially if the style of how an idea is presented becomes the main concern (style takes over substance).

PHILOSOPHY OF PRAGMATISM

Is there a non-value driven truth? Is it possible to seek any knowledge that is not guided by any interest whatsoever? The pragmatist account of knowledge states that any knowledge is a tool because of its instrumental function. Generally speaking, pragmatists believe that "truth" has a purpose to serve because it is always there to satisfy some particular interest and/or expectation.

Accordingly, epistemic truth is not discovered, but constructed in terms of its potential to "perform" consistently with the concerns, hopes, and wishes under which it was initially designed or pursued by the knowing subject. One might say that pragmatists ask the following questions: What is the cash value of knowledge or beliefs in experiential terms? Are there any practical applications for believing in X? Are there any potential uses if the belief is accepted as true?

Generally speaking, Pragmatic theory of truth states that no idea or belief is born true. "Truth" as "true belief" is a status that <u>is awarded to a belief</u> in accordance with the interests and expectations of the subject or the community.

CORRESPONDENCE THEORY OF "truth"

The correspondence theory of truth presupposes that there is an independent or objective reality that true beliefs "correctly" represent. Accordingly, knowledge as true belief is valid or legitimate insofar that it "corresponds to" this objective reality. In this context, "corresponding to" means that true belief captures some feature of an independent reality and hence, knowledge does not depend on human interests or expectations. This means that ideas are born true or false since the criteria for judging truth and falsity depend on the relationship that an idea or belief has to its corresponding entity in reality.

In this regard, since knowledge is a representation of some aspect of an objective reality, any philosophical claim concerned with the existence of something in the world and its changes would have to presuppose the correspondence theory of truth.

OBJECTIVITY OF TRADITIONAL PHILOSOPHY

The history of philosophy, dominated by metaphysics, is filled with endless discussions and claims about an independent reality relying on a kind of epistemology that would seek "objectivity." Richard Rorty, the prominent American pragmatist, calls traditional epistemology "objectivity" which represents for an external or transcendental point of view. Such a view seeks "objectivity" insofar that it aims to understand things as they are in themselves without requiring or presupposing a context or framework. In short, seeking "objectivity" is the epistemic attempt to see the world and everything in it without having any perspective whatsoever. It also means that epistemic truth applies the correspondence theory of truth and that unlike the pragmatist account of truth, the epistemic process or activity is NOT guided by any interest, expectation, hope, wish or other human concern, not even by social, cultural, political or historical factors. The person who seeks "objectivity" neither hopes for some advantage or benefit nor intends to capitalize on truth in the future. Accordingly, seeking knowledge for the objectivist has intrinsic value and not instrumental value, which is equivalent to seeking truth as an end in itself, and not for any application or mission.

TRADITIONAL NOTION OF "TRUTH"

The notion of "Truth" is the metaphysical truth, often spelled with capital "T". This is the metaphysical truth that is presupposed in the history of Western Philosophical tradition.   Since such truth is not man-made, it is considered as the ultimate, first or final truth, all of which can and have been widely interpreted. Although some philosophers interpreted this truth with capital T as God, many critical or non-religious thinkers interpret "Truth" as the essence of things. In the context of Plato's ontological dualism, the metaphysical truth is the form or idea that exists independently as an abstract, immaterial entity constituting the essence or being of things. Therefore a metaphysician who seeks "Truth" asks about the underlying principle that defines a thing.

ANTI-REALIST NOTION OF "truth"

In accordance with Rorty's account, the notion of truth with small "t" is the type of epistemic truth that pragmatists would seek. In contrast to the traditional view in epistemology, the pragmatist does not seek objectivity since no independent objective reality is assumed.

In other words, while metaphysicians of traditional philosophy often presuppose realism, the pragmatist account of knowledge presupposes anti-realism. Accordingly, NOT presupposing an objective independent reality translates into NOT seeking a true belief that corresponds to an objective reality. In this context, since the aim of epistemic activity is not about establishing a relationship between an object and how accurately it is represented, the truth and falsity of an idea is determined based on its practical applications (pragmatic theory of truth).

On Rorty's account, once values are identified, "the facts" can be determined. In accordance with what Rorty calls "solidarity" (pragmatist approach), the validity of a belief is judged by its ability to serve the community somehow.

All things considered, there is no need for a "sophisticated epistemology" since the true belief or knowledge depends on its ability to satisfy communal values or interests. The bottom line of a pragmatist account is that truth or falsity depends on what the community members can agree on since, strictly speaking, epistemic truth is entirely conventional. In short, Rorty's epistemology does not validate knowledge, but rather explains the validation of knowledge through conversation and agreement among a set community.

A NATURALISTIC INTRODUCTION TO PHILOSOPHY

DIFFERENCES BETWEEN TRADITIONAL PHILOSOPHY AND PRAGMATISM OF RORTY

While the pragmatism of Rorty defends the view that truth is determined by the needs and interests of the community, the truth and falsity of a belief in the context of objectivity (traditional epistemology) is determined by the correct application of the method. One might say that an Objectivist distances himself from persons around him by attaching himself to non-human realities using a special method or procedure (see Plato's allegory of the Cave, for example), while the pragmatist, one who seeks solidarity, searches for human relations and conversations that lead the community to a "better belief" insofar that it fulfils communal needs. This means that the pragmatist account of knowledge is descriptive, since it documents the social process under which an agreement (truth) has been reached. In contrast to such an account, the epistemology of Plato, Descartes and other Objectivists is concerned with the outcome of epistemic activity, is determined or dictated by the special method of the epistemologists.

All things considered, the type of epistemology that Rorty calls "objectivity" is normative, and based on the prescribed true belief which corresponds to TRUTH, while the solidarity of pragmatism describes the birth of true belief as that which is agreed upon within the boundaries of the community, without any claim that it corresponds to some non-human reality or entity.

DIFFERENCE BETWEEN NATURALISM AND OTHER FORMS OF ANALYTIC PHILOSOPHY

While Naturalism is an analytic philosophy, not all forms of analytic philosophy are naturalistic. For example, Descartes is known as the father of modern analytic philosophy but his epistemology is not naturalistic.

At this point, it is prudent to acknowledge the differences between naturalistic epistemologies and other forms of analytic epistemologies. The difference is based on the framework or the context in which a naturalized epistemology operates. An epistemology that claims to be naturalistic commits itself to work within the boundaries of science. In other words, a naturalized epistemology exclusively investigates within the limits of scientific framework. In contrast, Descartes' epistemology, in spite of its analytic approach, is committed to the framework of "reason" and its associated notion of "clear and distinct ideas"!

In fact, there have been a variety of analytic philosophies developed throughout history that were committed to frameworks other than science; hence, they were not naturalistic in spite of their occasional reference to science. The relationship between philosophy and science has been the subject of debate for a long time. Philosophers have discussed whether science should participate in philosophical investigations at all and if yes, how, but all philosophers agree that philosophy is not there to compete with science or replace science, especially when it comes to making factual claims. There is no doubt <u>that the authority or privilege of making factual claims goes entirely to science</u> due to philosophy's lack of proper methods and procedures to offer any alternative. Another topic of debate is whether or not it's possible to lead a meaningful and constructive philosophical discussion without relying on some factual claims of science. For example, how can philosophy investigate reality or daily experiences without including the reality that science has revealed to us, namely, the universe with its billions of stars, planets and distant galaxies that is approximately 13.8 billion years old?

All things considered, any serious philosophical investigation must either presuppose some scientific facts or must integrate its claims with already existing scientific claims, therefore it is unimaginable to practice philosophy without including scientific knowledge.

WHAT MAKES AN IDEA SCIENTIFIC?

In the previous section, it was explained that what distinguishes Naturalism from other forms of analytic philosophy is the commitment of Naturalism to operate within the framework of science. At this point, it is prudent to ask what the understanding of Naturalism about science is.

There are two accounts of science: normative and descriptive. The normative account falls under the domain of Philosophy of Science which is the traditional prescriptive discipline aimed at justifying scientific knowledge, establishing the reliability of scientific method etc. In contrast, Naturalism as an empirical and descriptive discipline aims at describing how scientific knowledge is "commonly" developed or how the scientific community has historically determined an idea to be scientific. In addition, a descriptive account does not only seek to understand the origins of scientific knowledge , but also how the understanding of science has changed over time, including what associated practices and activities we currently consider to be the leading criteria or standards for accepting an idea as scientific. Again, this naturalistic approach is fundamentally different than the attempt to validate knowledge claims in science, which would fall under the disciplinary interests of Philosophy of Science.

One commonly accepted view in our time is that science heavily relies on empirical methods, and it is safe to say that this method has proven itself as the most reliable method for developing factual knowledge. However, not all empirical studies are accepted as scientific. For example, many socio-cultural beliefs which are also known as "common sense" are developed through observations but are not scientific. In other words, although, experience is a necessary condition for an idea to be judged as scientific, it is not sufficient on its own.

Another standard seems to be that scientific ideas have potential for growth while non-scientific views do not. To unpack this characteristic a little further, let's consider some beliefs that have religious origin and no potential for growth. For example, creationism is a religious interpretation about the origin of life on earth and struggles badly to evolve while Darwinism as the alternative view has evolved significantly.

Here is another way to explain this difference: scientific beliefs are special kinds of "stories" in so far that they often grow over time as new or additional empirical tests are performed. In other words, a scientific belief is NOT an exceptional or an isolated belief limited to a particular time and place. Rather, a scientific belief can be tested and become more mature, meaning that additional empirical studies can reveal new aspects and potentially causal relationships, allowing for a detailed understanding of phenomena at hand.

The third characteristic is the ability to explain. Unlike other beliefs, scientific beliefs offer a "complete account" of the events, meaning that they describe how things happen from A to Z. In fact, the explanatory power of science is the dominant reason for seeking science in the first place: to understand why things happen <u>in step by step.</u> All things considered, an accurate and sophisticated scientific explanation improves and ultimately completes our understanding, which could not be achieved otherwise (see explanations of medicine for example concerning how diseases originate and spread within human communities). Such explanations could eventually describe how things change over time (i.e. how viruses change and adapt).

And finally, the most important characteristic for accepting an idea as scientific is predictability, meaning the very same explanations of scientific beliefs that describe changes also provide opportunities for predicting these changes. These explanations are often accompanied by the ability to control the process and manipulate the outcome. In fact, predictability and control have been historically the dominant criteria for judging ideas as scientific. For instance, the reason for why astronomy is accepted as science while astrology is not goes back to the undisputed fact that astronomy enables events to be accurately predicted.

COHERENCE THEORY OF TRUTH

Coherrentism refers to coherence theory of truth and it allows consistency among various scientific ideas, with "consistency" meaning the adaptability of an idea. In accordance with this truth concept, any newly proposed idea must be consistent with other ideas in science (scientific tradition) in order to be accepted as scientific. Having said that, the lack of consistency or adaptability criteria can be overruled or ignored if the predictability criteria were met. The "revolution" that came with quantum theory is a perfect example for how <u>predictability</u> can overrule the lack of consistency or adaptability of a proposed idea. Nevertheless, consistency with the scientific tradition has historically been a dominant criterion for accepting ideas as scientific, and it has been the center stage for developing theories, which are structures that demonstrate relationships between various components or ideas that are consistent with each other, thereby forming a "system" (developing a scientific theory is an attempt to create a system consisting of a network or web of many ideas that are complementary, as well as in coherent relationships with each other). What guarantees coherrentism within a system, or in this case a scientific theory, is the language of science consisting of mathematical descriptions. In other words, it is no surprise that math has been adopted as the standard language of sciences due to its ability to guarantee consistency among the ideas within a science by applying the coherence theory of truth.

WHAT IS MEANT BY "GOOD SCIENCE?"

First, it is important to note that the terms good and bad when used to describe science are not meant in the ethical or moral sense, but rather as either effective or ineffective. Further, a naturalistic account of "good science" does not prescribe the right approach or way of practicing science, but instead describes, based on the lessons of history, how an effective practice of science is identified. As far as reviewing the history of science and using it as a foundation to distinguish between good and bad science practices is concerned, the objective of such an attempt would be to specify what methods and procedures have led to "scientific progress" in the past. These methods can be in the form of producing constructive results, such as technological achievements, or in the form of enhancing theoretical sophistications by paving a path for further theoretical unifications. Either way, a naturalistic account aims at learning from the history of "successful practices" in science without prescribing any method or procedure on its own.

In the same token, a historical account might reveal practices that have delayed or distracted research at some point. Identifying these practices helps to minimize the chance of repeating them. In fact, it might turn out that learning from unsuccessful approaches, "bad science," is more practical than attempting to establish the "special qualities" of good practices in science.

A review of the practices of science from the 20th century shows that the so called "Nazi Science" was more committed to preserving and defending certain political assumptions, cultural beliefs and values instead of identifying and discovering underlying causal relationships. Interpreting or manipulating data, or directing the end results of an experiment to be consistent with political and ideological agendas, are examples of ineffective or bad practice of science. The problem with such practices is that they are not critical at all and hence not inquisitive, but rather loaded with agendas and plans to confirm or establish some "truth" that is introduced ideologically. Regarding "Nazi Science," protecting the cultural myths of Nazi ideology had priority over the predictability and control of events, which should be the standard guiding values of empirical sciences, as discussed previously.

Contrary to the aforementioned tendencies of ineffective practices of science, the history of science can also offer some examples of effective practices. Good sciences have often been "opportunistic" and "promiscuous" in their attempts to predict and control events, which in this context suggests that they are bold or "shameless" and do not pursue any agendas, nor are they committed to any principle, criteria or worldview whatsoever. To illustrate the <u>flexibility</u> of good science as described above, let's take a look at Quantum physics. In spite of the highly abstract nature and of the non-conventional views and assumptions of quantum physics, this theory is accepted as scientific because it is the best available tool for predicting events in the subatomic world, so far. The point here is that adopting unconventional beliefs requires a great level of flexibility, which is tolerated only because of expected predictability, control of events and increased explanatory power of the issues at hand promised by quantum theory.

All things considered, the good practice of science is neither committed to confirm any cultural or ideological beliefs and values, nor is it in search of some invisible, unchanging and eternal principles that transcend human experience. Rather, it is highly flexible when applied to an unconventional conceptual framework, assumption or non-traditional belief, as in the above description of good science with "opportunistic" and "promiscuous" traits.

A NATURALISTIC INTRODUCTION TO PHILOSOPHY

WHY IS THE SUBJECT AND THE METHOD OF NATURALISM TIED TOGETHER?

There are an infinite number of projects that could be pursued philosophically, just as there are an infinite number of questions that could be asked in an area of studies. As already mentioned in the first chapter, everything can be examined critically and hence, philosophically; as far as Naturalism is concerned, the purpose is to discuss and analyze "truth", which is defined by naturalists as "scientific truth *or a sort of truth that is "factual" and its validity can be established through scientific procedures."* This means that the method of Naturalism limits what can be examined naturalistically. For example, the areas like art and spirituality cannot be examined scientifically; hence, there is no naturalistic account of aesthetic.

One should bear in mind that although Naturalism as a philosophical view is pursued analytically, methodically and consistent with legitimate and respectful scientific studies and their results, it is not the purpose of Naturalism to promote "scientism" (whatever that means) or to scientifically justify certain beliefs and values. In contrast to traditional philosophy, Naturalism has no agenda whatsoever. Instead of pursuing some cultural or social objective, naturalistic philosophies aim to apply science critically to commonly pursued cultural beliefs and values, deconstruct unfounded and dangerous cultural beliefs and tendencies, and demystify superstitions, pseudo-scientific claims and mythologies.

At the same time, the Metaphilosophy of Naturalism challenges commonly pursued objectives in philosophy, such as the promotion of an ideology or religion, as well as intellectual views in academia, because many of them are valued solely for cultural reasons. For example, there have been too many instances in which the philosophies of Plato, Descartes, Kant, Nietzsche, Heidegger, and Kierkegaard (just to name a few) have been misused to support pseudo facts, cultural agendas, political views and gains, social domination, religious manipulations, and more, not to mention that some of the above listed philosophers practiced philosophy because they were motivated by their own personal and cultural agendas.

In contrast, although Naturalism, equipped with scientific knowledge and its critical and analytic tools has no agenda, it can be constructive in many societies by debunking cultural practices that are in conflict with human wellbeing, such as female circumcision. This ritual for example is still practiced and demanded by some cultures in Africa in spite of the well-known physical and medical risks, as well as the potential psychological trauma.

In summary, it is not the objective or purpose of Naturalism to prescribe values, life style, worldviews, preferences or anything else, but rather to make us aware of potential outcomes, side effects and consequences. Again, <u>prescribing truth or value is precisely what Naturalism aims to avoid.</u> In fact, any so called "scientifically based life style" or culture not only misuses science and undermines the integrity of critical and analytic research associated with Naturalism, but also risks becoming a form of demagoguery. In short there will be NO "normative science of values" that prescribes what individuals or communities ought to value; however, it is imaginable to have a science that describes how or perhaps why individuals and communities value what they value. A scientific or a psychological account of how values emerge or become popular socially (under specific circumstances), is not only conceivable, but also desirable for the purpose of maximizing critical analyses and understanding of causal relationships.

In the case of female circumcisions, a naturalistic account could go as far as revealing that there are no physical and psychological advantages at all for preserving this ritual, <u>although the choice or the judgment that this ritual must end cannot be demanded scientifically or naturalistically</u>. Ultimately, it will be the task or the choice of a culture to decide in favor of reform. Either way, a critical and analytic examination of this ritual backed by scientific knowledge could establish existing and non-existing causal relationships including all the participating factors, side effects, and outcomes, without the attempt to guide the culture into any specific direction or moral choice.

The task of promoting moral values and actions falls under the domain of traditional normative ethics and other associated normative disciplines, such as social political philosophy.

PROBLEMS FACING THE TRANSITION FROM NORMATIVE TO DESCRIPTIVE

Western philosophical tradition is characterized by the "critical examination" of issues, while thinking critically is understood as "reflective thinking". Russell, a prominent philosopher of analytic tradition, considered reflective thinking to be <u>the defining constructive contribution of Philosophy to humanity in general</u>. On his account, reflective thinking is a contribution in so far that it allows us to "see familiar things in an unfamiliar way."

What makes reflective thinking unavoidable in the context of examining issues critically is that without including and evaluating other perspectives or alternatives, one is neither examining nor investigating a problem, nor searching for any "truth". Therefore, a genuine investigation based on critical analyses requires that no stone is left unturned. In other words, reflective thinking is necessary to conduct an unbiased investigation that is committed to a critical outcome. This is the main reason that religious thinking is not considered critical, because religion is dictated and the "faithful" are warned about other religions and other perspectives in general. Examples of narrow-mindedness could also appear in a philosophical discourse when cultural commitments limit research, such as Euro-centrism, which has been defended by many philosophers in the past including the philosopher and theologian Immanuel Kant (1724-1804).

NATURALISTIC ACCOUNT OF A PRIORI ASSUMPTIONS

In the previous section, it was explained that a good practice of science has no ideological or cultural commitments and it is inclusive, flexible and creative in achieving its objectives of predictability and control of events, even at the cost of accepting or borrowing bizarre assumptions in the process. In fact, it was in this context that good science was considered to be opportunistic and promiscuous because it treats a priori assumptions instrumentally. Instrumental views of a priori assumptions maximize flexibility and adaptability of the approach, modifying and eventually replacing assumptions and ideas as needed or as the observational results suggest or recommend. For example, realism, or the assumption that an independent reality exists, has ONLY been instrumental for practicing a science that values predictability and control of the experienced daily reality. Again, what makes this assumption (realism) true is that it allows us to explain the consistency of our experience and develop a science as the result of that consistency. In other words, realism is NOT an achievement of science, proving that an external world actually exists separately from the mind in the Cartesian sense; however, <u>realism has been a necessary assumption for practicing good science so far.</u>

Earlier in this chapter, quantum physics was mentioned as an example of good science for the same reason, as it is indeed the most successful available tool for describing our physical system because of its demonstrated flexibility of replacing realism, which is expendable but has been historically the traditional assumption in science, with anti-realism.

As far as naturalistic accounts of a priori assumptions are concerned, since naturalistic accounts do NOT inject additional values or beliefs on their own, they simply inherit the same views held by effective scientific approaches. Accordingly, a priori assumptions are no longer presented as entities or principles or objects or a "thing in itself" (something that transcends human experience), but as expendable theoretical tools applied only to enhance sophistications of a theory in terms of simplification, generalization and unification.

WHY NATURALISM IS AT ODDS WITH EURO-CENTRISM

Naturalism was defined in the previous chapter as being critical, analytic and consistent with scientific findings and approach. In the above section, it was explained how thinking critically requires exhausting all available perspectives, as well as flexibility towards assumptions and values. Euro-centrism, the philosophical view that proudly refers to the tradition of Western philosophy which has supposedly given birth to "critical thinking", limits the extent to which thinking critically can be practiced. In other words, on one side the Metaphilosophy of Western philosophy is defined through its critical approach, while on the other side, Euro-centrism stands in the way of thinking critically about cultural commitments of Western philosophy itself. Consequently, Naturalism, which has adopted critical approaches for its investigations, must be at odds with Euro-centrism, as well as with any other form of ethnocentrism. To illustrate how the critical and reflective approaches of Naturalism are at odds with Euro-centrism, let's consider a maze as an analogy.

When it is determined in a maze that a route leads to nowhere, then that particular route must be abandoned so other routes can be tested. Analogously, in Naturalism, if it is already established that any form of Platonism has little, if any explanatory power regarding our experience and knowledge of the world today, then it must be abandoned as well.

Now, if Western philosophy were genuinely critical in the above mentioned sense, then the allegory of the cave, in spite of its "cultural values" and in spite of Plato's historical status in the Western tradition, would have been abandoned - but is it?

A NATURALISTIC INTRODUCTION TO PHILOSOPHY

Frankly speaking, the problem is not the story of the cave but the framework that comes with it, namely the commitment to metaphysics, realism, essentialism (Euro-centrism). Although this philosophical framework of Plato's allegory was an accomplishment for its time and many centuries after that, it does nothing today aside from glorifying the tradition. Nevertheless, it has been kept academically relevant solely for cultural and historical reasons. In short, the commitment to Euro-centrism is the only plausible explanation as far as why philosophers have been struggling so long with abandoning, naïve, superficial and expired philosophy of Platonic ideas.

USE OF LANGUAGE IN THE CONTEXT OF NATURALISTIC PHILOSOPHY

Since Naturalism as a form of empiricism has its roots in the framework of analytic philosophical tradition, special attention to its use of language is a MUST. This means that plausible explanations are needed for why a linguistic term is introduced or repeatedly used by the author. These explanations have to be either linked to some kind of experience, such as x represents something in the factual world, or they must have some "practical application," such as x is a useful theoretical entity, similar to the instrumental use of a priori assumptions as discussed above.

Either way, in the context of a naturalistic account, linguistic terms cannot be taken for granted, and references to tradition, cultural agenda or projects, such as revealing secrets of "pure reason", are not sufficient unless there are indications that these notions are linked directly or indirectly to some human experience and hence they are NOT self-serving metaphysical entities.

In order to offer a naturalistic account and to make the transition from a normative to a descriptive framework (naturalizing), the language in which philosophical questions are formed must originate from the linguistic framework of a science such as physics, chemistry, or psychology. For example, the question concerning the essence of DNA is not a scientific question and as a result, it cannot be addressed naturalistically by taking advantage of biology. One could perhaps talk about the molecular structure of DNA or its chemical combination, but not its "essence". Similarly, questions such as what constitutes "the being" of an electron is a metaphysical and not a scientific question. Generally speaking, metaphysical terms such as substance, form, being should be avoided entirely in naturalistic language.

This does not mean that only scientific questions can be answered naturalistically. For example, the question "what IS a human being?" has historically been a philosophical question concerned with the nature or defining criteria for "being human". The problem with this question is that it is presented or formulated normatively, meaning the question only accepts normative claims as answer. To offer a naturalistic account, this question must be reformulated, for example, "What are the differences between humans and animals?" The answer in this case will be both descriptive and empirical, allowing the use of psychology, other social sciences and natural sciences to DESCRIBE how humans are a different kind of animal. In short, "naturalizing" an account requires that we edit questions in such a way that they can be answered scientifically.

In some instances, it seems that naturalizing an account could translate to taking the lead in scientific research, for example, by asking questions that have not been asked before because we have not found a way to rearrange questions in such a way that they could be answered descriptively and empirically. There are some cultural myths that demand that certain issues can only be addressed normatively!

WHY NATURALISM?

As stated, Naturalism stands on the shoulder of sciences by taking full advantage of scientific knowledge and methods; however, Naturalism is not limited to what sciences have said about a particular topic so far. Naturalism is an inclusive philosophical view as long as ideas are developed critically and are not in conflict with established scientific facts, although it is important to note that scientific approach is both critical and analytic. Above all, there is no argument as to why we should exclude scientific facts when we are engaged in philosophical activities, not to mention that sciences have become a standard part of human life and experience and it becomes increasingly more difficult, if not impossible to exclude scientific facts and observational methods of science.

 In addition, it is safe to say that there are unique qualities about Naturalism compared to other "isms" in philosophy. For example, it transcends cultural boundaries because it is not limited to any culture such as east or west, European, Chinese, or African. Naturalism is also unique because it is not limited to any time period of human history. It has and will continue to survive cultural and historical changes in contrast to other philosophical views that usually "come and go", meaning that they become popular for a decade or perhaps a century, but eventually become history. Contrary to other "isms", Naturalism is here to stay because humans depend on science for survival, but also because science continues to provide constructive results. Scientific frame work has been more constructive, as well as historically more dependable than any other framework that philosophical views have been using for their normative claims (cultural, linguistic, social, religious, etc.).

Another advantage of Naturalism is that traditional problems in the epistemology and philosophy of science, such as skepticism, are no longer present. This is the case since the traditional method of justification for normative claims is replaced by standard scientific method of justification for descriptive claims.

Finally, naturalizing, or the transition from normative to descriptive framework, seems to be unavoidable for many philosophical disciplines, including metaphysics and epistemology. To illustrate this further consider the following analogy.

Similar to the fact that children will grow and seek independence regardless of their parent's approval, it is historically unavoidable that normative disciplines at some point reach their "intellectual maturity" by completing a transition to a descriptive and empirical frame work. Analogously as "good parents" prepare their children for their future; it would be the task of a successful naturalistic account of science to prepare the existing normative disciplines of epistemology and philosophy of science to make their transition into a scientific framework.

In this regard, as "bad parents" don't contribute to development of their children and sometimes sabotage their growth purposely just to keep their children close at home, <u>it cannot be the objective of any normative philosophy to keep disciplines in their normative frameworks for as long as possible.</u> Since transition from normative to descriptive has occurred before with disciplines like psychology, cosmology, and anthropology, a naturalistic account of science could actively contribute to these types of transitions.

Chapter 7

Naturalistic Account of Science and the Prospect of Emerging the Discipline of Naturalistic Studies

Unlike the normative disciplines in philosophy, such as Philosophy of Science, a naturalistic account of science aims at describing the origin of science scientifically. Having said that, describing how scientific knowledge is possible cannot be separated from how any knowledge gathered through experience is possible, unless one demands a "special status" for the type of empirical knowledge developed in science. In this regard, normative demands for a special status for explanandum, in this case scientific knowledge, would require a metaphysical approach and would not be consistent with naturalism. Therefore, knowledge relying on experience must be accounted for scientifically in order to explain how scientific knowledge originates from an observational method of science. What this means is that a naturalized epistemology would have to precede any naturalistic account of science.

As explained in the previous chapter, the transition from a normative discipline to a descriptive one has occurred before and it may be considered the norm when a normative discipline gains methodological sophistication, as it recently did with anthropology.

It's important to note that there have been serious attempts to naturalize normative disciplines before and this is nothing new. In fact, David Hume was perhaps the first naturalist to seek a naturalized epistemology by offering a psychological account of causality.

In our time, W.V.O. Quine has been a prominent figure of naturalistic views. His project, introduced in his article "Epistemology Naturalized," quickly became influential in the circle of analytic philosophy. Quine's project is ultimately the same as the Humean project in that it relies on the psychological reconstruction of knowledge because rational or logical accounts of science failed, especially by positivism.

According to Quine, the objective of naturalized epistemology is to describe and explain the birth or the origin of science instead of seeking a validation or "justification" of science through arguments within the framework of the traditional normative approach.

Since epistemology and philosophy of science are not the only normative disciplines that will make their transition to a descriptive framework, the question becomes if a special discipline should be developed and devoted to accelerate these types of transitions.

In this regard, it is to propose "The Discipline of Naturalistic Studies" that has the objective of creating a transitional path by which normative disciplines become independent sciences. Such a discipline would serve as a stepping stone by helping different branches of philosophy evolve in to an independent science by replacing their a priori assumptions and beliefs with empirically based concepts in a descriptive setting. In short, while naturalism as a special philosophical approach offers different competing perspectives that are critical, analytic and consistent with well-established scientific facts <u>without preferring one perspective over another,</u> the proposed discipline of naturalistic studies <u>has a specific disciplinary interest</u> as described above.

Based on the above mentioned so far, although there are overlaps among various fields of studies listed below, there are also boundaries between them as far as their disciplinary interests and methods are concerned:

1. Philosophy
2. Naturalism
3. The proposed Discipline of Naturalistic Studies
4. Science

The following diagram visually depicts the boundaries and overlaps and aims to illustrate the disciplinary interests of the Naturalistic Studies. It is important to note that the diagram below should not be used to interpret how disciplines are structured methodically or should be classified (positivism, for example, is a descriptive and not a normative account of knowledge).

Accordingly, Naturalistic Studies has a clear agenda to lead normative disciplines to transition into new, descriptive frameworks, while Naturalism as a philosophical view (as understood here) offers descriptive and empirical views of various issues, while being critical and analytical about the claims associated with these issues <u>with NO agenda</u>.

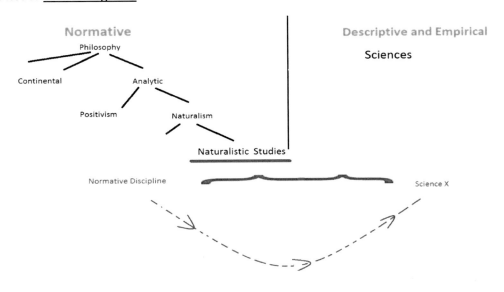

As the diagram shows, Naturalism is a form of analytic philosophy and hence inquisitive or highly critical and careful with its use of language. This means that although naturalism has no agenda of its own, it is also NOT committed to preserving cultural myths, values and beliefs.

For example, Kantian philosophy, which relies on the notion of "vernunft" will be challenged because sciences such as psychology have not discovered "reason" or "vernunft" in the world. Furthermore, it is unlikely that there will be any empirical evidence or indication from other sciences that would suggest the presence or influence of "pure reason".

In summary, as predicted, epistemology in particular will become an independent science at some point, regardless of how philosophers (like Kant) may attempt to delay these types of transitions by reiterating their strong commitment to *a priori* philosophies with normative claims.

THE RELEVANCE OF LOGICAL POSITIVISM FOR THE DISCIPLINE OF NATURALISTIC STUDIES

The greatest contribution of logical positivism to the development of naturalized epistemology was that it set the stage for the analytic framework that made it possible for naturalized epistemology to exist. First, positivism demonstrated the historical problems of a priori epistemologies (more on that later). Second, positivism elevated the importance of the philosophy of science, and of science in general, for the future of philosophy as such and epistemology in particular. Third, if one can speak of "a positivist turn" in the history of philosophy around the early to mid-twentieth century, it opened the door for descriptive epistemologies to exist alongside of the traditional normative epistemologies. In this context, naturalized epistemology as a form of descriptive epistemology benefited greatly as well.

In regard to the first point, namely the reckless use of a priori concepts and beliefs in philosophy, positivists established that language was misused in the history of philosophy by metaphysicians (see Ayer's thesis in Language, Truth and Logic). Accordingly, many problems in philosophy are pseudo-problems caused by the overuse or misuse of a priori concepts and by the careless use of language in general. In addition, from a positivist point of view, since there is no truth or fact of matter that transcends experience, positivism promotes a form of empiricism, like naturalism, as well as seeking an anti-realist account of knowledge like any naturalized epistemology.

Further, the metaphilosophy of positivism defined the purpose of philosophy at least partly by exposing metaphysics and its associated mistakes and or pseudo-problems. This project was radical in its core because it demanded the elimination of metaphysics all together, which was referred to as "ending conceptual confusions."

Further, the task of philosophy was defined by positivists as analyzing and clarifying the language of science. This was called "conceptual analysis," since it was aimed at analyzing the use of and meaning of scientific terms. Specifically, the objective was to translate the language of science (theoretical language) which has cognitive meaning and hence can be true or false to observational language. By doing so, the objective was to achieve clarity.

In other words, the conceptual analysis can be understood as an attempt to re-write or more effectively express complex, abstract scientific statements to make them more clear, specific and meaningful statements of observational language.

Although positivism ultimately failed with its intended projects, (including a rational reconstruction of science, Ayer's principle of verifiability agendas, etc.), it succeeded in the discrediting of metaphysical projects. One might even say that "the elimination of metaphysics" was made possible because of well-developed attacks by positivism, as well as the ability of positivism to deconstruct unfounded assumptions, arbitrary beliefs, and the sloppy, ill-defined language of metaphysicians.

Finally, due to the special attention of positivism to the use of language in philosophy by demanding clearly defined terms and methods, positivism left its legacy by contributing to development of an analytic framework used to set the stage for naturalistic studies.

SOME DIFFERENCES BETWEEN POSITIVISM AND TRADITIONAL PHILOSOPHY

The main difference between positivism and a-priori-driven normative traditional philosophy is that positivism is concerned with language and not about the make of things. Positivists are not concerned with the nature of "the experienced" or its essence, but rather with the language used to describe what has been observed or experienced. Perhaps Positivism can be understood as the most radical form of empiricism since from the positivist point of view, philosophy becomes linguistic, while the traditional approach of normative philosophy ceases to exist. For example, positivism presupposes anti-realism and anti-essentialism for its empiricist account, in contrary to traditional empiricist views of normative epistemology which often presupposes realism and essentialism for their account of knowledge.

NATURALIZED EPISTEMOLOGY

A Naturalized account of knowledge includes a scientific account of how knowledge is constructed through experience, as well as what "happens" to that knowledge socially and culturally. In other words, as long as knowledge is not factual or scientific, the process through which knowledge is accepted or adopted in a community and how it spreads socially and culturally must be examined. For example, a naturalistic account would seek psychological explanations for how individuals might consider a belief to be true despite the absence of any evidence, and why they would reject a "belief" in spite of the overwhelming amount of evidence.

The explanation of how ideas are judged as true or false may presuppose unconscious cognitive activities or motives through which an individual is more receptive to accepting a belief as knowledge, such as promoting self-value, affirming self-worth or expecting pleasure, and perhaps rejecting an idea as true due to fear of potential harm or loss of power and influence. In other words, from a psychological point of view, knowledge claims always have an instrumental or practical purpose that they serve while beliefs that no longer serve their originally intended purpose become unfounded, unjustified, false, misrepresented, or even morally wrong. Such accounts might be able to answer the earlier question of why individuals might refuse to accept a particular belief as true in spite of the overwhelming amount of evidence, namely that the belief no longer serves its intended objective. It is in this context that the "true belief" will be demoted from its status of knowledge to false belief, and no evidence will be sufficient or solid enough to prevent that.

Further, the reference to evidence, including the use of logic or "reason", becomes ad hoc since the choice of accepting a belief happens prior to introducing "supporting rationale". In this case, the epistemologist goes shopping for evidence, instead of the evidence convincing the epistemologist to accept an idea as true.

Consistent with the above naturalistic explanations, even philosophers may have had psychological motives, such as religious and cultural, for promoting or rejecting various beliefs to preserve the beliefs, concepts and theories with which they were personally familiar, or with which they had cultural associations and emotional attachments. For example, consider Kant's "twelve" categories and Descartes's meditations, to name a few.

Although naturalistic accounts assign instrumental value to knowledge claims (knowledge has a specific function to serve), they still value scientific facts intrinsically. For example, it is a fact that the universe is approximately 13.8 billion years old and therefore, it is valued intrinsically in a naturalistic framework. On the other hand, the knowledge claim that Pluto is a planet (or not) and therefore worthy of closer study is valued instrumentally; if we want to understand the origin of our solar system, we have to know what is happening on this planet/Kuiper belt object.

Another way of expressing this distinction is to say that since facts are unchanging, they are valued intrinsically, such as the earth is round and not flat, and water is made of one oxygen and two hydrogen atoms, while naturalistic accounts that are consistent with scientific knowledge but perspectival are valued instrumentally, as it is not moral, for example, to continue with female circumcision if we want to preserve and protect human well-being.

All things considered, a naturalistic account of knowledge ultimately seeks a factual claim about factual claims. Whether or not this is possible remains open or unanswered at this point, although there is no reason to believe that there cannot be facts about how facts are discovered (unchanging psychological conditions of the human mind through which facts are produced).

WHAT DOES IT TAKE TO HAVE A NATURALIZED ACCOUNT OF KNOWLEDGE?

As the above diagram shows, the discipline of naturalistic studies has several objectives, such as assisting normative branches of philosophy with their transition to a descriptive and empirical framework by outlining the steps for these disciplines to evolve into an independent science. Further, it is the objective of this discipline to offer a scientific account of science, a process that could possibly lead to unification of all sciences by demonstrating the relationship between all sciences.

Although this adventurous and ambitious objective is not achievable in the immediate future, it can begin with the objective of offering a scientific account of how non-scientific empirical knowledge originates, including how individuals develop various types of knowledge through experience or observation on daily basis. Any scientific account of this kind would have to be based on the link between observation and knowledge in order to psychologically demonstrate the origin of "true belief" from A–Z. As already indicated, since psychology is theoretically the most equipped scientific discipline, as well as uniquely positioned to integrate and unify all theoretical concepts of the human mind into one process, it should take the lead in seeking a scientific account of knowledge.

In this regard, the relationship between the theory of mind and the theory of knowledge deserves special attention. This relationship could be imagined like the relationship that a system (theory of mind) has to its subsystem (theory of knowledge).

Again, the attempt to naturalize epistemology is NOT about the "validation of knowledge" (Kantian type of project) but rather a descriptive (psychological) account of HOW knowledge is developed. Accordingly, the completion of a psychological account of knowledge is only possible if a sophisticated understanding of the inner working of human mind already exists.

Ironically, seeking a psychological account of knowledge may accelerate research in cognitive psychology and other cognitive sciences, and therefore lead to a better understanding of the human mind, hence to a more mature psychology. Further, by bundling the focuses of various areas of psychology in to one specific project, new theoretical tools or concepts may be developed by which psychology is led into forming a coherent structure that binds transitional relationships between the various branches of psychology. This means that by developing a more sophisticated theoretical framework, psychology would come one step closer to its ultimate vision of becoming the science of the human psyche.

A naturalistic account of knowledge in the discipline of psychology requires a complete description of how factors such as emotions, cognition, etc., in conjunction with social, cultural and other environmental factors, participate in the origin of any empirical knowledge in general, and scientific knowledge in particular.

Accordingly, an ideal naturalized theory of knowledge that is equipped with detailed contributions of other sciences, like sociology, history, anthropology, medicine etc., would have to be able to explain how humans arrive at knowledge psychologically, how they validate beliefs as knowledge, how communities preserve and defend beliefs as true, and the conditions in which they begin to challenge these beliefs.

All things considered, although the proposed discipline of Naturalistic Studies will take full advantage of all scientific knowledge and methods available, its research and "activities" remain "philosophical" and not scientific. Its inability to become a scientific discipline is due to the lack of standardized methods and procedures that would enable its transition from a normative to a descriptive framework. Above all, the proposed discipline of Naturalistic Studies always operates cognitively on the meta-level of the discipline in question; therefore, it has no prospect of becoming a science itself despite that its disciplinary interests are entirely devoted to science.

USE OF A PRIORI CONCEPTS IN THE CONTEXT OF NATURALIZED EPISTEMOLOGY

Virtually all cultures embrace unfounded beliefs, values and claims about the world, which are often manifested in form of a priori assumptions in their respected philosophies. Many of these beliefs are accepted uncritically and passed to the next generation as hand me down beliefs and perspectives of the world. These passed down beliefs provide the framework of traditions that are celebrated and glorified by a culture, and in particular by the philosophers of that culture, often for many centuries.

Therefore, it is no surprise that some of these beliefs and values are injected directly or indirectly as a priori assumptions in to the belief systems that arise from the traditions.

The commitment of Western culture to define knowledge as "representative" would be an example of a Western a priori assumption, and it would explain why all Western epistemologists refer to either empirical or a priori representations. (Representations as cognitive constructs are thoughts that can be written down or lectured, and hence communicated and discussed through language.)

This particular a priori assumption of Western tradition has prohibited Western scholars from examining other types of knowledge, such as intuitive knowledge, which is also called non-representative knowledge.

Since naturalized epistemology is free from cultural commitments, at least explicitly, although some could still sneak in, it cannot ignore other possible definitions of knowledge, such as non-representative or intuitive knowledge promoted by virtually all non-western epistemologies. This means that naturalized epistemology is more inclusive compared to normative epistemologies in which a priori assumptions are embedded in their cultural framework, struggling to detach themselves from their prescribed, unchanging definitions. Further, since the use of non-western epistemic notions in the context of naturalized epistemology is permissible, this flexibility adds to the reflective and critical approach of this epistemology.

In summary, the strong attachment of normative epistemologies to their underlying cultural beliefs stands in their way of examining other perspectives, which is required for thinking reflectively and critically. In contrary to normative epistemologies, the flexibility of naturalistic epistemology in regard to adopting non-western a priori assumptions provides additional options for thinking reflectively, and its origin can be traced back to the flexibility of practicing good science as discussed in the previous chapter.

In the context of seeking naturalized epistemology, a priori assumptions will be replaced by empirically based assumptions later; however, a priori assumptions seem unavoidable, at least in the initial process of transitioning any normative epistemology into its new footing. Unlike the traditional epistemologies that interpret their a priori assumptions as some sort of "self-evident necessary truth," or, "entities representing some underlying principle of reality" of some kind, in a naturalistic framework a priori assumptions are expendable tools introduced only with the intention of being replaced by descriptive and empirical concepts in the future. In the context of naturalized epistemology, a priori assumptions are there to serve as crucial steps only in so far that they "jumpstart" empirical studies, and their validity expires as soon as empirically based concepts become available. As an analogy for the use of a priori assumptions in a naturalistic setting, consider how the first stages of rockets are jettisoned (a priori assumptions) as soon their fuel has burned to the end.

DOES NATURALIZED EPISTEMOLOGY DE-WESTERNIZE EPISTEMOLOGY?

The short answer to the above question is: Yes. Having said that, de-Westernization is NOT the same as "refuting" Western epistemology, but rather involves removing the dominant inflexibility that has been injected into Western metaphysics and epistemology by Western cultural belief systems throughout history. As it was partly suggested in the previous section, de-westernization is important, or maybe necessary, for any naturalized account of knowledge because its critical setting requires thinking reflectively, hence transcending Western cultural framework. Accordingly, the attempt to transcend Western cultural boundaries means expressing disloyalty to Western cultural belief system and values, which is interpreted here as de-westernization. On the other side, looking at "de-westernization attempts" constructively would mean that epistemology can be naturalized only if epistemology becomes a trans-cultural empirical study like astronomy, physics and psychology. As we don't have "Asian astronomy" or "South American physics" or "Eastern chemistry", we wouldn't have Western epistemology, Eastern epistemology, and African epistemology, as it is currently the case, but instead we would have one trans-cultural empirical study with the potential of becoming "the Science of Knowledge".

An inclusive or trans-cultural epistemology is required in order to maximize the critical and creative approaches needed for epistemology to evolve further and become a "Science of Knowledge". It may sound ironic to say that, for its own sake, Western epistemology should be liberated from the cultural assumptions that it has imposed on itself uncritically throughout history.

PHILOSOPHY, NATURALISM AND THE DISCIPLINE OF NATURALISTIC STUDIES

As it was explained in the first chapter, the purpose and method of Philosophy remains undefinable due to many available and competing options that are all appealing, yet with no universal or cross-cultural consensus to have as a final answer.

Naturalism is not clearly defined in academia and its understanding depends entirely on the naturalist, or the philosopher who considers him or herself a naturalist, but what all naturalists would have to agree on is the need for consistency with science. In this regard, making factual claims falls under the domain of science and not philosophy.

In addition, it was stated earlier that naturalism is to be defined based on its method and not its purpose, since there are no socio-cultural agendas, projects or objectives that are "reserved" specifically for naturalists. However, it may be a constructive use of the critical and analytical approach of Naturalism to expose charlatans and demagogues, unmask pseudoscientific claims and demystify cultural myths.

It is the goal of this book to insist on a distinction between the proposed discipline of Naturalistic Studies and "Naturalism", in spite of the overlaps concerning the desired and applied methods. In other words, while the discipline of Naturalistic Studies is derived from naturalistic philosophy in a sense that it applies the same critical and analytical approaches and relies on consistency with science, the discipline has its own specific agenda or well defined objective, namely to substitute the normative frameworks of various philosophical disciplines with descriptive and empirical frameworks.

All things considered, in contrast to naturalism, the discipline of Naturalistic Studies pursues specific objectives; hence it is more than just an analytic and critical evaluation of various ideas consistent with science. Since it lacks a standardized or methodical approach, it falls short of being a scientific discipline. In other words, the Discipline of Naturalistic Studies differs from Naturalistic philosophy because of its purpose and doesn't operate as a scientific discipline because of its method. Having said that, there is no reason why the discipline of naturalistic studies could not learn from the historical success of "good practices of science" as mentioned in the last chapter and adopt flexibility in regard to the use of a priori assumptions to reach its disciplinary objectives.

The following chapter will examine what a potential naturalized epistemology might look like and what problems or issues would have to be overcome. In this regard, the objective of the next chapter is not to actually offer a naturalized account of knowledge, but rather to explore some obstacles and challenges facing the development of a naturalized epistemology. Although such an account will be experimental, it might shed light on how the mission of the discipline of naturalistic studies could be completed.

Chapter 8
Setting the Stage for a Naturalized Theory of Knowledge

As it was explained in the previous chapter, the objective of naturalized epistemology is to seek a scientific account of knowledge. This effort is consistent with Quine's attempt at a psychological reconstruction of science, which can be understood as an extension or modern version of the Humean project.

As indicated by Quine, a naturalized account of knowledge would be a psychological account of knowledge which includes the study of cognitive activities responsible for the construction of knowledge, and the cognitive activities required for monitoring and regulating the entire process of knowledge formation.

This chapter is intended only to hypothesize what a naturalized account might look like; the proposed account serves only as a possibility and is not an actual proposal of a naturalized account of representative knowledge. Regardless of how the naturalized epistemology may look in the end, it will be subject to constant modifications and changes as empirical sciences progress. *In other words, there will be no final version of naturalized epistemology because future scientific changes will impact the entire understanding of science and any explanations arising from it.*

WHY EURO-CENTRISM IS THE FIRST GREATEST OBSTACLE FOR NATURALIZING EPISTEMOLOGY

In accordance with Western tradition, knowledge is defined only through the presence of a representation or idea in the mind, which is marked by the debate between empiricists and rationalists over which type of representations (empirical or a priori) are more dependable. In spite of this debate, both theories of knowledge agree that it takes a representation to have knowledge, but the notion that knowledge is defined exclusively as representative has been only an a priori assumption of Western tradition.

Any naturalistic account of knowledge would not only have to challenge this historical Western perspective of knowledge, but also why the idea of intuitive knowledge was pursued in a very limited way in academic dialogues about epistemology (see knowledge by Acquaintance by Russell). Western epistemology exclusively considers Western understanding of human experience, which is a Eurocentric approach and is not a sufficient reflection philosophical understanding of knowledge.

In the context of discipline of Naturalistic Studies, the "cure" for this narrow-minded form of ethnocentrism is inclusivity. Accordingly, no interpretation or view should be ruled out or prejudged because of its non-Western cultural associations. This means that any assumption can be adopted a priori as long as it can answer the following question: *What assumption or concept must be accepted a priori in order to initiate the inclusion of empirical studies within the normative framework of a particular philosophical discipline?*

In the end, regardless of which a priori assumption is selected, it would have to be replaced by a descriptive view that has an empirical origin in psychology and or other cognitive sciences.

WHY A PSYCHOLOGICAL THEORY OF KNOWLEDGE?

Since the notion of observation has enjoyed a higher degree of relevance and "prestige" with natural sciences than it has with social sciences (empirical studies such as physics have served historically as models for empirical studies in social sciences), it can be claimed that a naturalized account of knowledge falls primarily under the domain of cognitive psychology rather than linguistics. Cognitive psychology and linguistics both rely on observations; however, psychology develops its knowledge from empirical data, which is gathered directly from experience.

Furthermore, achieving a successful naturalized account of knowledge using theories of mind from psychology to develop explanations about how representation of an object is constructed is more likely than using a coherent demonstration of propositions that could be offered in a linguistic framework.

Why seek a naturalistic account of knowledge at all? The answer would have to be that the traditional normative epistemology that relies on an objectivist realist account has proven to be a MYTH, and is naively grounded on epistemic assumptions, such as human values and interests, as well as social, historical and cultural factors all of which could be eliminated or ignored (this has been THE MYTH of Euro-centrism reflected in the epistemologies of Plato, Descartes and Kant).

An alternative to the realist position in epistemology would be an anti-realist view of knowledge that would include human interests and values, but only by demonstrating their involvement in the process. Any theory of knowledge that includes human interests and values in its account would have to be psychological; this is the main argument in defense of a naturalized epistemology. There are unavoidable social interactions that would shape the conditions for seeking knowledge, and it is the objective of a naturalized epistemology to reveal those conditions. Such naturalized accounts could look like social epistemology of Alcoff, or the feminist epistemology of E. Anderson. Alcoff and other social epistemologists claimed that epistemological activities remain social and political in their core, so as long as there are guiding social, cultural, political or even personal interests shaping the process of knowledge formation, psychology as the science of the human psyche must be involved.

TAKING THE FIRST STEPS TOWARD NATURALIZED EPISTEMOLOGY

A naturalistic account of knowledge aims to describe the origin of knowledge, from the first known psychological activity that initiates the process of knowledge formation to its completion. A brief sketch of what the process may look like is shown in the diagram below, which illustrates how a possible motive, such as valuing power or feeling important, leads to a particular mental representation that constitutes true belief. This implies that true belief is somehow instrumental for physical, psychological or socio-cultural survival of the person claiming that knowledge. For example, valuing self or self-worth / self-esteem could be a psychological reason for judging an idea to be true.

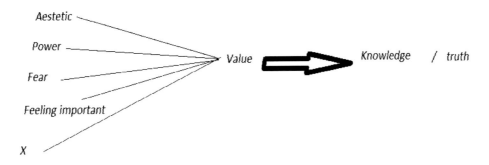

To test this empirically, a hypothesis may be presented that individuals who have "high levels of self-esteem" are more likely to judge the views of others as true, while individuals with "low self-esteem" have a tendency to judge other people's views as false. Obviously, the correlation between an individual's self-esteem and the opinions of others is not that simple, and there are multiple factors involved. Predictions that involve evaluating individuals' tendencies to judge ideas as true or false are very complicated and remain challenging in spite of extensive research in psychology. Nevertheless, the existing models could be enhanced further. What is known as "jealousy" could be explained by an individual feeling less valuable or worthy because of highly valued qualities that are present in another person or persons. In this regard, the jealous person might not be aware that he or she has a tendency to judge others as incompetent. In this case, a psychological model is needed that could predict (with high probability) certain degrees of receptiveness or willingness among individuals to accept or reject beliefs. This type of model is needed because individuals are more receptive to ideas, beliefs or values that have the potential to increase their self-esteem, making their life more "meaningful" (see patriotism, nationalism or other forms of ethnocentrism / tribalism). As a result, extensive empirical studies are needed in order to prepare, develop and enhance the processes for profiling individuals and predicting their behaviors. With enhanced processes, experiments could be conducted based on predictions; for example, individuals with a common history and past experience will find their self-value or self-worth likely in x, y or z, and as a result, these individuals will be more receptive to ideas and values that affirm or promote x, y, z.

For another example, consider the following statement: *Our poets, and writers, our athletes and scientists are the best because the success of our nation is mine, too, and the glories and accomplishments of our nation and its past history, adds to my self-esteem.* In this case, the tendency to judge certain ideas or individuals is DIRECTLY linked to the probability of experiencing an increased self-value or pride. The bottom line is that individuals' unconscious cognitions tend to agree with certain cultural claims based on the assumption that national and/or cultural "success" is transferrable to members of that culture.

Finally, accepting a belief as true due to expected increase of self-value explains why most new ideas face social and cultural resistance at their start. New ideas appear threatening because they challenge our confidence, raising doubts about the traditions and beliefs of our native culture. These traditions psychologically reassure us that we are entitled to our socio-cultural privileges and rights, making us feel comfortable with ourselves, our worldviews, our daily judgments, but also guaranteeing our self-worth or self-value.

APPLYING PROBLEM SOLVING RESEARCH IN PSYCHOLOGY TO EXPLAIN THE ORIGIN OF REPRESENTATIONS

In the previous chapters, we learned that traditional epistemology defines knowledge through representations, or in other words, "knowing" is a mind activity constituted by representations that are either a priori or empirical. In this regard, any psychological theory of knowledge will describe how mental or cognitive representations originate.

The following hypothetical descriptions serve only as examples of the issues a naturalized epistemology could face in its attempt to synthesize a complete scientific account of knowledge. In this context, terms such as proposal, hypothetical or prototype will be used to emphasize the experimental nature of the challenges that a successful naturalized epistemology would have to overcome. By introducing potential issues and solutions, the following proposal could assist with expediting the development of a sophisticated psychological theory of knowledge, while clarifying what naturalistic explanations of representative knowledge could possibly look like.

To simplify potential naturalistic explanations, we will refer to mental constructs as "mental objects", and when they are accepted as true, we will refer to that object as "representation". This means that a naturalistic account would have to scientifically describe at least two processes:

1.The process through which a mental object (potential representation) is developed, and 2) the process through which a mental object is accepted as a representation of the object represented ("object represented" is the object, entity, person, etc. in the world or the awareness of the object made possible through experience).

In other words, representation is <u>a status </u>that it is "awarded" to a mental object because the mental object is accepted as the correct mental image of the experienced object.

Accepting a mental object as "representation" of an object represented means that a naturalistic account would examine the social, cultural and other psychological factors involved in evaluating, judging and ultimately assigning representation status to that mental object; therefore, considering a mental object as "representation" is a value judgement about the proposed mental object.

A NATURALISTIC INTRODUCTION TO PHILOSOPHY

Distinguishing the above two descriptive processes that must be accounted for scientifically suggests that while the conscious and intentional activities of the mind are responsible for cognitively constructing a mental object, declaring that mental object as "representation" might depend on external constraints that an independent reality imposes on the process, and rely on subject's reasons for seeking the knowledge claim in the first place.

If no specific strategies of thinking can be identified psychologically, either for constructing a mental object or for judging the mental object as "representation", then a psychological account of knowledge would instead demonstrate the influence of common sense or daily knowledge in origination of the mental object and its acceptance as representation. A naturalized epistemology would have to provide a psychological account of how daily knowledge or other forms of non-scientific knowledge change over time, as well as how this type of knowledge (non-scientific) may be involved in shaping knowledge production in science. Any form of a psychological account aimed at the origination of a mental object and its "approval" as representation will be explanatory and not justificatory. Such accounts would have to be consistent with already-existing theories in psychology and associated sciences, and they would also have to include descriptions and analyses using standard scientific language and approaches, such as experimentation and induction. For example, to explicate the origin of a mental object by adopting the descriptive language of sciences, there is a whole range of available cognitive studies and research in psychology, including "problem solving," that could be applied for this purpose.

In the context of problem solving, the entire cognitive process from start to finish would have to be interpreted as a solution to a specific problem, for example, <u>which mental object could be representative for the experienced object, event or change in the world.</u>

In layman's terms, "thinking" initiates and monitors problem-solving activities while "the problem" consists of determining which mental object would satisfy the guiding interests and expectations of the subject.

Herbert Simon (1972) studied problem-solving activities in the context of the information processing system (IPS). Simon holds the view that the studies of problem solving contribute to the understanding of how thinking occurs. His empirical studies of problem solving portray a mechanistic picture of how such activities take place. Although Simon's studies fall short of providing a comprehensive and unified account of the problem-solving activities of the human mind, they offer a detailed and broad empirical examination of the various determinants and mechanisms involved.[1]

---

[1] Since the problem solving proposal introduced here asserts that the mental object reflects the interests of the subject (the interests of the subject vary case by case), the cognitions of the subject (problem solving activities) would have to aim at how these interests could be achieved. The process of how the mental object originates could be broken down into many steps, and each step could be examined and studied independently. For example, the first step could be how to define the problem. Sternberg (2003) discusses the difference between well-defined and ill-defined problems. His distinction of classifying problems states that a "well defined problem" has a relatively trivial path to its solution and an ill-defined problem does not. Further, an ill-defined problem might require multiple solutions as well as an unclear and unspecific path for pursuing a solution. In addition, Sternberg (1985) constructed a theory that explains the regulatory function of a meta-level executive cognitive process for planning, monitoring, and evaluating the problem-solving process. His theory aims at explaining problem recognition, definition, and representation by demonstrating how the problem-solving process is guided by the meta-level activities of the mind. This would mean, for example, that a scientific account of the mental object, which could define the origin of the mental object as a problem-solving activity, could further expand its explanations by including Sternberg's theory of meta-level cognitive processes.

Other issues facing a psychological account of the mental object may arise regarding the medium in which the activities of the mind occur. For example, could language be considered as a medium for "thinking"? Does thinking (constructing a mental object) occur through language? And if linguistic operations are involved, do cognitive strategies for problem solving processes depend on language and its flexibilities?

Several notions and issues would have to be addressed scientifically if explanations for the above questions were to be developed in to a naturalistic account of knowledge. These notions and issues include "thinking", "medium for thinking", "linguistic operations available within the framework of language", "cognitive strategies used for problem solving" (constructing a mental object), "guiding interests of the thinking subject" and, "external constrains that an independent reality imposes on the process."

Led by psychology, a complete naturalized account would also seek interdisciplinary explanations, not only with social sciences but also with natural sciences, like neurosciences, in order to include bio-chemical activities of the brain in its explanations.

JUDGING TRUTH AND FALSITY OF A KNOWLEDGE CLAIM

In accordance with the above proposed problem solving account, any judgment about the truth or falsity of a knowledge claim begins with a judgment about a mental object. Since there are many possible mental objects (potential representations) that could be considered, the question concerning which mental object is the "accurate" or the true mental image of the object represented will depend on what function or ability is expected from that particular mental object. In the context of the problem solving approach, if the mental object serves the interests of the problem solver, then the mental object is true and becomes a representation of the object represented. In other words, any judgment about the truth or falsity of the mental object would require an understanding of the purpose of the knowledge (see pragmatic truth concept).

Although the process that creates a mental object and the process that makes a judgment about truth and falsity of it are linked, the attempt to construct a mental object does not guarantee assigning a truth value to it (awarding representation status to the mental object). What this means is that different individuals who have the same interest may not have same expectations as to which mental object best serves their guiding interests.

However, the guiding interests of the subject are not the only factors that determine which mental object is qualified; subjects also have expectations that serve as a regulatory function for selecting which mental object performs best.

For example, in a scientific community, not all scientists have the same level of expectations concerning predictions and or explanations of a particular theory (see the historical struggle of quantum theory in the previous century).

Although the problem solving theories could help explain the construction of a mental object, the real challenge lies in judging or evaluating various competing mental objects and determining whether or not they qualify for representation status. As already stated both processes are linked, but the process of accepting or rejecting a proposed mental object as the solution to the problem could be heavily influenced by social, political, cultural, religious and other communal factors. For example, for the question of what causes mental illness such as schizophrenia, possible competing mental objects could include demons, God's will, genetic factors, biochemical factors, and more.

SOME COMMENTS AND CONCLUSIONS CONCERNING THE PROPOSED PSYCHOLOGICAL ACCOUNT OF REPRESENTATIVE KNOWLEDGE

From a philosophical standpoint regarding a psychological account of knowledge, since the cognitions of the subject guide the thinking activities responsible for the origination of representations, representations are conceived internalistically. This is true because the mental object is the result of the consciously directed cognitive activities of the subject. Unlike externalist views internalist accounts indicate that what epistemizes belief is constituted by the means that are accessible to the cognizer from the standpoint of first-person consciousness.

What has not yet been discussed in the proposed psychological account is the state of the "object represented". In the context of naturalism, any intersubjectivly verifiable appearance can be considered as an object of experience; seeking a scientific account explains why the object appears the way it does. This understanding allows for a detour that not only avoids skepticism, but also prevents associated metaphysical dilemmas, such as the Cartesian problem concerning the "existence" or "reality" of the experienced appearance.

Consistent with the instrumental use of a priori assumptions in the context of Naturalistic Studies (see chapter 7), the object represented can be "treated" as an independent object, meaning that it exists independently from the interests, wishes, beliefs and abilities of the subject, but only in so far that it makes a scientific account of its representation possible.

In other words, although the object represented is understood realistically, namely as an object that exists independently from the subject's beliefs or judgments, a naturalist account of knowledge aims at describing how the physical, bio-chemical as well as psychological conditions of the subject influence the appearance of the object to the subject. (For more discussion concerning a naturalistic theory of experience, see chapter 9 "Naturalistic Account of Reality: Prospects of Developing a Psychological Theory of Experience as an Alternative to Kantian".

DIFFERENCES BETWEEN THE PROPOSED PSYCHOLOGICAL AND THE TRADITIONAL REALIST VIEW OF KNOWLEDGE

This proposal emerges from the premise that the relationship between a representation and object represented is actively constituted by the judgments of the subject; without this judgment, there is no relationship. Specifically, it exists on pragmatic ground, hence, semantic irrealism; this kind of relationship is defined in irreducibly normative (epistemic) terms such as good belief, warranted assertiveness or rational belief, or irreducibly normative (moral or aesthetic) terms such as human emancipation, flourishing or well-being. In short, since the proposal's interpretation of what determines the relationship is defined normatively (in accordance with the interests and expectations of the subject), the relationship between representation and object represented can be classified as semantic irrealism.

In contrast to the proposed account, traditional realist views of knowledge presuppose semantic realism in the Cartesian sense, where truth is defined as a non-normative, non-epistemic relationship between propositions (statement, sentence) and some state of affairs or fact. In this case, an object represented is understood as the object in the external world and the cognizer will have no ability to shape or determine the reality of this object.

Since realist accounts of knowledge use correspondence theory of truth, they often fail to explain what constitutes the relationship between a representation and its corresponding object in the world; this indicates that the subject might not have access to what makes this relationship possible. This means that many realist accounts defend the externalist theory of truth because the truth-maker is not accessible to the subject (semantic externalism). Externalist theories of truth maintain that that what makes a proposition, assertion or belief true (its truth-maker) need not be accessible to a cognizer from the standpoint of first-person consciousness.

Chapter 9
How a Naturalistic Account of Reality Could Look

PROSPECTS OF DEVELOPING A PSYCHOLOGICAL THEORY OF EXPERIENCE AS AN ALTERNATIVE TO KANTIAN

ABSTRACT

It is the intention of this section to establish the need for an alternative theory to the Kantian theory of experience, and to propose a path with which an alternative theory could be developed by psychology. Such a theory should be able to offer an entirely scientific description of all activities that lead to the birth of an appearance called "the experienced object." It is not the intention of mine to refute Kant's theory of experience, but rather to claim as part of the overall argument of this article that Kantian theory has outlived its abilities to provide explanations for post-Newtonian physics, and since a psychological theory of experience can take advantage of newly emerging scientific concepts and theories as they become available, it can evolve and gain more sophistication over time; hence, it is more promising than the Kantian theory relying on normativity and *a priori* concepts.

The position of Kantian philosophy in the history of western tradition is well known. Kant's philosophy has also received a great amount of attention and recognition worldwide, even by scholars who have challenged Kant's conclusions, assumptions and style of philosophy.

In fact, it is not an exaggeration to say that for many centuries to come, Kant himself will be remembered as one of the most influential philosophers of all time. In particular, his theory of experience introduced in *The Critique of Pure Reason* is undoubtedly the most sophisticated theory of experience that has ever been developed and available to this day.

It is the primary objective of this section to offer several reasons that should establish the need for an alternative theory to the Kantian theory of experience, and secondly, to propose a path under which this alternative theory could be developed by psychology and other cognitive sciences. While establishing the reasons for an alternative theory by pointing out the problems associated with Kant's theory, we will determine what can be learned from the Kantian approach in the first Critique that is necessary to construct the proposed psychological theory of experience.

In regard to the above-mentioned objectives, it is not the intention of this section to "refute" Kant's theory of experience but rather to claim as part of the overall argument of this section that Kantian theory has lived out its abilities to provide explanations for post-Newtonian physics. Specifically, it will be demonstrated that Kant's theory is unable to explain certain types of experiences that are possible in today's laboratories due to recent theoretical achievements in science.

Further, this article makes the claim that since a psychological theory of experience can take advantage of newly emerging scientific concepts and theories as they become available, it can evolve and gain more sophistication over time; hence, it is more promising than the Kantian theory relying on normativity and *a priori* concepts with little or no room for further growth and development.

As far as how the success of this grand project can be determined in the end, it is to say that a <u>successful psychological theory of experience should be able to explain how objects as appearances are possible by offering a detailed demonstration of all activities of the mind through which the presence of an object in consciousness can be accounted for psychologically.</u> Such an account is equated with <u>an entirely scientific description of all activities that lead to the birth of an appearance called "the experienced object."</u>

KANT'S THEORY OF EXPERIENCE

Immanuel Kant developed his theory of experience in his work *The Critique of Pure Reason*, published in 1781. In this work, Kant defended a special account of realism claiming that the experienced world exists "independently" from the wishes, interests, beliefs and evidential practices of the observer. Kant's primary concern in the first critique was to establish the conditions under which 'something' can be $_{REAL}$ for us, while to be $_{REAL}$, according to Kant means something that can be experienced by our senses. It is in this context that Kant's theory of reality becomes identical with his theory of experience. In other words, Kant claims that the mind is structured in such a way that only $_{OBJECTS}$ can be real for us because only $_{OBJECTS}$ can be experienced by our senses, meaning that for something to be known based on experience, it must be an $_{OBJECT}$.

Kant constructs his theory of experience or his theory of reality normatively in the context of his philosophy called *transcendental idealism* by arguing that since $_{EXPERIENCE}$ cannot relate objects to thoughts arbitrarily, $_{EXPERIENCE}$ must relate objects to thoughts in <u>a pre-established *a priori* fashion</u>. The Kantian argument in defense of the pre-established *a priori* conditions of experience can be summarized by saying <u>that while sense data can be considered as content of experience, the mode or how the sense data is presented cannot be considered content because</u> $_{EXPERIENCE}$ <u>cannot organize its own mode</u>. It is on this ground that Kant identifies, establishes and explains the pre-established $_{MODE\ OF\ EXPERIENCE}$, including the *a priori* intuition of time and space as conditions under which something can be an object of experience and therefore real for us.

All things considered, Kantian metaphysics spells out the conditions of experience and considers them to be conceptual features of experience, setting the framework not only for the occurrence but also the consistency and reliability of $_{EXPERIENCE}$ as such. Further, Kant claims that he has shown in the Critique that since the world cannot be otherwise for us than as we are experiencing it, our experience of the world is consistent, and our understanding of it, justified.

It will be shown later in this section that even if Kant did succeed in demonstrating a justified account of experience, his theory is unable to offer a complete account of all possible experience in science, and because of this limitation there is a need for an alternative theory of experience.

WHAT IS THE KANTIAN METHOD FOR DEVELOPING HIS THEORY OF EXPERIENCE?

The Kantian method to constructing his theory of experience in the Critique can be summarized by stating that Kant applies various *a priori* concepts normatively. While he develops each of these concepts carefully and methodically, his theory becomes increasingly dependent on additional *a priori* concepts to bring all the thus-far developed concepts together, creating SYNTHESIS and UNITIES.

As already stated, what stands out in the first Critique as the crucial assumption of transcendental idealism is that since only objects can be experienced, only objects can be known, but the notion of OBJECT / MOVING OBJECT as subjects of mathematical descriptions in time--space happens to be a metaphysical assumption of Newtonian physics as well. Although this similarity does not establish that Kant's theory of experience is a custom-designed theory of experience in defense of Newtonian physics, it does indicate that Newton's theory might have been some inspiration for Kant.

If it is true that Kant's inspiration from Newtonian physics was an essential part of his approach, it is important to understand how the Newtonian views could have influenced the design of Kant's theory. One possible way to imagine this influence would be that the leading question for Kant in the pursuit of his theory of experience was: *How must a theory of experience be designed if its objective is to explain the Newtonian notion of experience as well as guarantee the legitimacy of the knowledge that is derived from it?* or *What theory of experience would be necessary in order to have a justified account of the Newtonian notion of* EXPERIENCED OBJECT *and its changes in time--space?*

All things considered, there are reasons to believe that Kant's approach in regard to developing a theory of experience was aimed at seeking consistency with Newtonian realism from the beginning, but also at providing a justified account or validation for it (as opposed to the Humean predicament of epistemological skepticism). In short, the importance of Newtonian physics for the Kantian method in the first Critique is analogous to a sort of compass that guides the overall development of Kant's theory to its final version.

Another aspect of the Kantian method is its reliance on a sophisticated theory of mind for his theory of experience. It is certain that Kant develops both his philosophy of mind and his theory of experience *a priori*. There are indications in the transcendental aesthetic that Kant develops his philosophy of mind parallel to his theory of experience, and obviously it was not the intention of Kant to act as a psychologist exposing or identifying the structure of the human mind, but rather that he "goes shopping" for a philosophy of mind that would be necessary for his theory of experience. In this case, Kant prescribes the structure of the mind in terms of his theory of experience by pursuing questions such as *How would the mind have to be structured if its operations are the a priori features of experience?*

In summary, it may be claimed that Kant develops his theory of mind normatively and *a priori,* and it was the Newtonian notion of ₑₓₚₑᵣᵢₑₙ𝒸ₑ𝒹 ₒᵦⱼₑ𝒸ₜ EXPERIENCED OBJECT as explanandum that set the stage not only for his theory of experience, but also for what philosophy of mind he would have to presuppose in order to have a "custom designed" theory of experience for Newtonian physics.

WHAT CAN A PSYCHOLOGICAL THEORY OF EXPERIENCE LEARN FROM THE KANTIAN APPROACH?

Unlike the Kantian approach, it is part of the overall claim of this article that it falls under the domain of psychology to construct a theory of ₘᵢₙ𝒹 MIND. Such a theory would have to be linked to a theory of experience that is also developed empirically and descriptively (psychologically). The relationship between these two theories can be represented through a relationship that a system (theory of mind) has to its subsystem (theory of experience), while the link between these two would also have to be accounted for descriptively and empirically (scientifically).

Although a psychological theory of experience would have to be pursued differently than the Kantian theory, there is one particular lesson that psychology can learn from the Kantian approach. This lesson consists of the leading question that Kant aimed to answer in the context of the first critique, and it can be formulated as follows: *How would the mind have to be imagined or "invented" if its operations have to be compatible with the conceptual features of "the way" we experience the world?* Based on this question, Kant pursued a philosophy of mind that is not only consistent with his theory of experience but also envisioned by him from the beginning with the purpose of providing a foundation for it.

As already stated, Kant applies a similar approach for developing his theory of experience based on his inspiration from Newtonian physics, and it is therefore no surprise that Kant identifies the *a priori* intuitions of time and space as conditions of experience as they were essential features of the Newtonian realism (understanding of the physical world).

The lesson that psychology could learn from the Kantian approach consists of seeking a theory of mind that is guided by similar Kantian types of questions, such as *How would the mind have to be imagined or "invented" if its operations have to be compatible with the structure of an empirically developed theory of experience?* In this context, since it is the psychological theory of experience as subsystem that deduces the "inner working" of a prospect theory of mind (the system as whole), the approach would have to be normative. Using a computer analogy, it would be similar to the question of what hardware requirements are needed, including what operating system such as windows 7 or windows XP, in order to install particular software on a computer. In this case, the software stands for the activities of the subsystem and the required hardware capacity and operating system for the system as a whole. The bottom line is about the potential applicability of the so called "Kantian approach" in the Critique: *What theory of mind would an empirically developed theory of experience have to require or demand in order for its own activities to take place?* Regardless if this so called "Kantian approach" proves itself to be fruitful for psychology or not, one is certain that an empirically developed theory of experience at the minimum will be a crucial stepping stone for a complete description of the inner workings of the mind, which is and has been "the most important disciplinary interest" of psychology in general. In other words, developing a psychological theory of experience will reveal itself as essential in completing the long pursued vision in psychology of becoming a science of the human psyche.

WHY SEEK AN ALTERNATIVE THEORY OF EXPERIENCE TO KANTIAN?

As stated implicitly in the introduction, the emergence of new theories in physics has provided some difficulty for Kant's theory of experience. Unlike Newtonian physics that correlate to the Kantian realist account of experience, the quantum theory has established in various ways that the interests, choices and conceptual framework of the observer cannot be excluded (anti-realism). In the following, it will be pointed out that the recent trend in scientific studies demands the collapse of the Kantian / Newtonian notion of experience to which we are accustomed. Along with this challenge, Kant's theory of experience is unable to explain the gap in regard to the quality of experience that is apparent between how electrons as objects of a quantum type of observation are experienced, and how trees as the objects of our scale of reality are experienced. Specifically stated, in the world of subatomic particles, electrons, unlike the objects of our everyday experiences, seem to exist based on the choices or conceptual understanding of reality that the observer has prior to and during the observation. Accordingly, what the observer aims to know shapes the conceptual framework of the observer about reality, which in turn influences the conditions of experiment (experience), and with that, what will be observed in the end (dualism of electron; if electron appears as particle or wave).

In other words, while consistent with the traditional or familiar notion of experience (Newtonian / Kantian) which is grounded on realism, the epistemological interests of the observer are irrelevant because the observer's conceptual understanding of reality will not influence the conditions of any experience, while on the contrary, "the quantum observations" suggest that the epistemological interest of the observer, such as knowing the location or knowing the momentum of an electron at a particular time constitutes the experiencing itself and its outcome, which is whether an electron behaves as particle or wave. Using Kantian language, this means that Kant's theory of experience is unable to explain why an electron is intuited differently compared to other empirical intuitions, such as a tree (while the location of an electron at a certain time cannot be determined, as is the case with some experiments in quantum physics - see Heisenberg's uncertainty principle - the location of a tree can be determined at all times).

In contrast to the Kantian theory, a proposed psychological theory of experience should be able to explain these differences due to its demand of a shift in the thus-far dominant conceptual framework of reality by replacing the realism of Newtonian physics with a conceptual understanding of reality that somewhat includes the perspectives, interests, and abilities of the observer (Anti-realism). In accordance with an anti-realist theory of experience, there is no neutral way of seeing the world because there is no interest-free or unbiased way of observing the world (the "realist promise" that it is possible to experience the world free from the interests, wishes and beliefs of the observer, although historically the most attractive view in the western tradition, is perhaps only a myth).

WHY WAS THE KANTIAN VIEW NOT REALISTIC TO BEGIN WITH?

In the previous section, I demonstrated how the Kantian theory of experience collapses in the light of the challenges that quantum physics has created for the Kantian theory of experience, which in turn explains why an alternative theory of experience is needed. In this section, I aim to point out why the Kantian theory of experience was not as realistic as Kant believed it to be.

First, it must be pointed out that Kant's theory of experience is developed somewhat linguistically because it relies on *a priori* concepts and definitions that he develops normatively, but also through deductions within the framework of his carefully developed language. In this context, Kant presents the language of the first critique as a medium that can reflect on how the experienced reality is structured by *a priori* intuition and concepts of the mind, but the crucial point is precisely this: Kant's hidden and erroneous assumption that the language of the Critique can expose objective features of the experienced reality. In short, Kant is not entitled to assume this capability from his language unless he has demonstrated this capability first, but Kant fails to demonstrate that the language of his philosophy (transcendental idealism) is neither social nor cultural; therefore, in the absence of such demonstration, Kant's linguistic analysis cannot be understood and judged as realistic. In other words, if language is exclusively a social entity, then it is embedded in a social, historical and ultimately perhaps cultural framework from *which it can never free itself because the language is "the product" of these types of communal activities.* This means that Kant has overlooked the social, historical, cultural and perhaps other contextual aspects of his language when he implicitly assumes that the language of the first Critique is somehow exceptional and therefore capable of fulfilling a realist account (capturing the objective features of reality that are independent from values, interests, hopes and wishes of the experiencing subject or observer).

All things considered, in our post Kantian era dominated by the philosophy of language of the twentieth century, it is legitimate to ask how valid the Kantian claims still are in regard to revealing the demands and agendas of "the pure reason," especially if the method that is used for such revelations (Kantian language) is not established by Kant as "pure" (non-cultural / non-social).

One might raise the objection that no philosopher in the history of metaphysics has ever taken upon himself the challenge of establishing "the objectivity of his language" in the above-mentioned sense (non-cultural / non-social language), but this is precisely the point of this article as well, that any realist account of experience would be flawed because *there is no possibility of developing a metaphysical language that is free from social and cultural commitments, including values, interests and so forth.*

In summary, because of the inconsistency of the Kantian approach with its own methods and claims (not being able to offer a realist account of experience, although demanded), but also because of the shortcomings of Kant's theory of experience in explaining the differences between the types of experiences in our scale of reality and the types of experiences that quantum physics has made possible, there is a need for seeking an alternative theory to Kant's theory of experience.

WHAT MUST BE ACCOUNTED FOR PSYCHOLOGICALLY?

It is part of the overall claim of this section that a comprehensive theory of experience should be able to explain how different individuals experience " the same situation" or same object differently, but also why an object appears the way it does in its unique way, with all its apparent physical features. To this end, an anti-realist framework is the best suited framework because only in such a framework can interests, values and other subjective and inter-subjective factors that constitute the experience of an appearance be accounted for at the expense of disregarding overly ambitious Kantian objectives, such as exposing non-cultural, non-historical and non-social conditions and features of experience.

To highlight the contrast between a realist and an anti-realist framework, one may say that while a metaphysical or normative theory of experience is concerned with questions including what is actually or really THERE (what is the invisible or underlying nature or essence of the appearance that exists independently from the mind), an anti-realist theory of experience will be concerned with the inter-subjectively verifiable descriptions that can be accounted for or explained scientifically. Further, in accordance with an anti-realist account, Cartesian questions such as if the appearance is even THERE in the world (does it really exist or is it just a hallucination) are not a priority as they are in a realist framework.

As far as why an anti-realist theory of experience must be predominantly psychological, the answer would be that since psychology among all sciences has the most potential to develop the most sophisticated anti-realist theory of experience in the long run, it is the science that should take the leadership for this project (a psychological theory of experience is the proposed theory in this section that ideally replaces Kant's metaphysical *a priori* and normative theory).

In regard to the question *what must be accounted for psychologically?*, the answer would be *a complete description of how subjective factors such as emotions, cognition, etc. in conjunction with inter-subjective factors such as social and cultural as well as other environmental factors participate in "the experiencing process" and ultimately shape the outcome of it, namely the conscious awareness of "the experienced object."* And precisely due to this potential ability of psychology to include, integrate and unify all the factors into one process, psychology is theoretically and conceptually the best equipped scientific discipline to develop the most detailed descriptive account of experience in the future, and hence is uniquely positioned among the sciences for taking on this project in an anti-realist framework.

It is crucial that a psychological theory of experience as a descriptive theory, unlike the Kantian theory, focus on the origin of "the perceived appearance" as a state of awareness rather than the origin of "the experienced object;" otherwise, it risks becoming a normative theory.

In other words, unlike the Kantian theory of experience, the center stage of a psychological theory of experience would have to be a descriptive account of a world made of "appearances" and not a world made of "objects." This means that a psychological theory **cannot permit** the standard or usual metaphysical "reality – appearance" distinction. In this context, metaphysical terms such as "essence" of …, "nature" of …, "being" of…. must be avoided; otherwise, the theory implicitly presupposes an "invisible reality" and hence becomes a normative theory. Above all, even the notion of $_{\text{EXPERIENCE}}$ itself is ironically too vague and was neither defined nor explained clearly by empiricists; it is therefore a metaphysical term that must be avoided as well.

This brings us to another important aspect of a psychological theory of experience, which is paying *special attention to the use of language* consistent with the goal of *describing* and not *prescribing* the activities of the mind. Specifically, an analytic approach is fundamental for a psychological theory of experience due to the accuracy of its language preventing additional assumptions or premises to sneak in, thereby compromising the empirical (not *a priori*) attempt of the project. As far as whether the project of constructing a descriptive theory of experience is feasible considering the current advancement in psychology, the answer at this point is unfortunately no, although there are various theories of perception in social psychology that could be part of this grand project or contribute somewhat to the development of a psychological theory of experience. These theories are focused on how individuals perceive the same situation differently. They include unconscious individual beliefs, hopes, wishes and expectations as well as individual tendencies to judge and interpret social situations, either learned culturally or based on personal past experiences in their account, to explain how *things are perceived subjectively* the way they are. For example, the Theory of Perceptual Set developed by Brunner and Postman at Yale University (1951) is one of these theories. This theory describes how beliefs and in particular individual expectations determine the perceptions of an individual in a social setting. In accordance with this theory, $_{\text{PERCEIVING}}$ is an active and not a passive process, as many realist theories of perception in psychology used to believe.

Considering the complexity of the task of developing a comprehensive psychological theory of experience as laid out above, it is impossible to predict when all the theoretical components, methods and tools will be available, but we can be certain that science does not happen on its own; it must be actively pursued by determined researchers continuously over a long period of time. Taking physics as an example, how long did it take before it reached the level of sophistication that it enjoys today? How many physicists from how many countries were involved in the process? Similarly, developing a science of the human mind, and with that a comprehensive scientific theory of human experience, will require a long journey and may require many centuries to come before it reaches the level of sophistication that physics possesses today concerning the natural world. Having said that, the groundwork can be laid in our time by:

1. Realizing that the Kantian theory of experience has been a temporary solution all along and it has outlived its abilities.

2. Accepting that a comprehensive theory of experience must be developed scientifically, which is only possible if it is developed in a framework that is descriptive, analytic and empirical, unlike the Kantian framework that is *a priori* and normative.

3. Introducing initial steps that would be required for the transition from an *a priori* normative framework to a scientific framework by redefining terms as well as applying a philosophical method or approach to serve as a stepping stone for achieving the objective.

These types of transitions were not unprecedented in the past. One could argue that there has been a historical trend regarding such a relationship between philosophy and science, namely that these transitions were and are recurring patterns and by no means exceptional. For example, Cosmology, Psychology and Anthropology were practiced normatively and often *a priori* for centuries, while today they are now operating in entirely descriptive and empirical frameworks as sciences. The reasons are partly obvious, namely that as the normative disciplines of philosophy evolve and become more sophisticated, they form their internal structure, system, and methodology for examining the problems that are embedded in their disciplinary interests. Most likely, the same development can be expected in the future for metaphysics and epistemology regardless of how strongly philosophers like Kant drag their feet trying to delay these developments by reiterating their strong commitment to *a priori* philosophy with normative claims (see the Kantian stand toward David Hume's type of epistemology). Further, such developments are unavoidable not only because the above-mentioned historical trends suggest so, but also because the newly emerging sciences continuously provide the possibility for new types of experience.

To illustrate this further, let's examine the relationship between newly emerging science and technology and "new types of experiences" briefly using some trivial examples like the electronic microscope, the Hubble space telescope, and infrared and X-ray telescopes. In all these cases, as physics became more sophisticated, it led to new technology and the new technology to new types of experiences (by "new type of experience" is meant not previously available or possible kinds of experience). This relationship is actually part of a cycle that begins with newly emerging science making new kinds of technology possible, and often the new technology, as we have seen repeatedly in history, can lead to the possibility of having new (not previously available) types of experiences (such as virtual reality), and as often claimed by empiricists, new experience leads to new knowledge and sometimes to new science, completing the circle that has begun with an emerging new science opening the door for unforeseen technology.

This apparent never-ending repetition of science challenging the notion of experience might also challenge the notion of "the thinking mind" every time a new kind of experience becomes possible, pushing for a new understanding of the human mind and its activities such as "sensing" and "doubting," and perhaps also pushing the demand for a new or modified theory of experience as well. The most visible example would be virtual reality technology. In regard to the rapidly advancing virtual reality technology, a whole range of questions appear. While some of these questions remind us of familiar Cartesian questions, some of them are "new breeds" of questions (categorically not previously existing), questions such as what are the differences between empirical knowledge based on "real experience" (non-virtual) and the empirical knowledge based on a "virtual experience," and further, what do both types of experience (virtual and non-virtual) have in common? What are their differences? And above all, do we need two different, distinct theories of experience?

THE PATH TO A PSYCHOLOGICAL THEORY OF EXPERIENCE

As stated and elaborated in the introduction, the purpose of a psychological theory of experience would have to be a scientific demonstration of mind activities through which the presence of an appearance in consciousness can be accounted for. Although it would be counterintuitive to prescribe how a scientific theory of experience should look or even be developed, it is probable that the transition from a normative to a descriptive theory of experience would require at least two phases. Again, it is not the intention of this article to prescribe how such a theory should be developed, but it is the intention to set an example for how a descriptive theory of experience could possibly be developed. Realizing that this is a weak claim, a little more explanation about the development of a descriptive theory of experience as an alternative to Kantian is in order, besides just demanding it here in this article.

As it has been already proposed thus far, the framework for a scientific or psychological theory of experience would have to contain three crucial features:

1. Descriptive
2. Empirical
3. Analytic

To prepare the groundwork or to set the stage for a framework that contains the above listed features, the following examples should serve as an eye-opening demonstration concerning a potential path for developing a psychological theory of experience. In other words, the following demonstration should only be understood as a *possible* practical approach for initiating scientific research in this direction. Accordingly, there are two phases needed for completion of this project. The first phase is to be called the "pre-scientific phase" and the second phase is to be called the "scientific phase" (with each phase is meant a transitional process that elevates the level or improves the quality of the above-mentioned features: descriptive, empirical and analytic). One could say that through each phase a potential theory of experience becomes more descriptive, more empirical and more analytic, hence more scientific.

The objective of the first phase (pre-scientific phase) would be to prepare an analytic framework by adopting a language that is psychological and contains definitions that are descriptive. Setting an analytic stage is important because it allows additional empirical concepts from various scientific disciplines to join the process through which they are integrated into the framework of the emerging psychological theory of experience. The second phase (scientific phase) will stand on the shoulders of the previous phase (pre-scientific), aiming at minimizing the use of *a priori* concepts and normative definitions that were unavoidable in the first phase. Despite psychology taking the lead with developing a descriptive empirical account of experience in the second phase, the process should not be limited to psychology. A psychological theory of experience should be accompanied by detailed explanations provided by other sciences, from the neurosciences and medicine to physics and biochemistry documenting all the micro activities involved within the brain.

All things considered, since the envisioned transition from *a priori* to empirical accompanied by the transition from normative to descriptive will depend on the sophistication of the existing theories in psychology and other related sciences at hand, it is unlikely that these transitions could occur abruptly. This means that it might require many phases through which the transition gradually becomes possible. Each phase serves as a stepping stone for the next phase using fewer *a priori* but more empirical concepts. This means that *a priori* concepts and assumptions are crucial for completion of the project in so far as they are instrumental in filling the potential gaps where they exist (in this context, "gaps" is defined as the lack of empirical concepts). Since the use of *a priori* assumptions is very central for completion of the project, it is necessary to elaborate on this a little more.

In context of a naturalist account of experience, *a priori* assumptions are a necessary evil designed to serve as stepping stones in order to jumpstart science, and their utilization expires as soon as empirically based explanations are available to replace them. *A priori* concepts are simply there to smooth the path to a truly scientific account of knowledge shaped by psychology.

Regarding a psychological theory of experience, *a priori* concepts are unavoidable especially at the initial stages of the first phase, but the objective should remain to replace these assumptions by descriptive and empirical judgments as sciences further evolve. Unlike traditional / normative philosophy, in the context of a naturalistic philosophy *a priori* assumptions are no longer treated as self-evident, eternal, non-human entities or truth that either are or represent some "underlying reality," etc. Instead, they are <u>expendable tools</u> or instruments only that are introduced with the intention of being replaced by descriptive, empirical (scientific), and in particular psychological concepts at some point in the future.

The way *a priori* assumptions and concepts are used in a naturalistic framework would look like the following: What assumptions or concepts must be accepted *a priori* in order to jumpstart scientific studies? Since there is currently no guideline, nor will there be any guideline or method in the future as far as what idea or concept must be assumed *a priori*, the only available options are trial and error, or the imagination of the theorist to propose an *a priori* concept creatively, but perhaps some level of luck factors in as well, coming together to introduce "the right" or necessary *a priori* assumptions and concepts in a particular theoretical encounter.

In addition, the use of *a priori* notions is important for answering other relevant epistemological questions, namely how do we know that the transition from a metaphysical to a scientific framework has taken place and if it is complete? The answer would be, when all *a priori* notions are replaced by empirically-based concepts and definitions that are descriptive.

The question is if a scientific account of "a science of experience" could ever be completed to the point that no *a priori* notion will be necessary. Unfortunately, the answer has to be "no" for the simple reason that the cycle of new technology making new types of experience possible will continue indefinitely, and consequently the completion of a final theory of experience becomes impossible.

In summary, as new science generates new knowledge making new technology possible, the new technology will unavoidably lead to a new kind or type of experience (a not so far existing form of experience), which in turn demands revision or replacement of a thus-far established theory of experience. Now it is in the context of the new theory of experience that *a priori* notions will become necessary again and so forth… It is the example of the dog chasing its tail because any final scientific breakthrough opens a new gate for admitting the design of a new science that is going to replace the expiring one. All in all, prioritizing this project for psychology (actively pursuing a psychological theory of experience) as already mentioned will be beneficial for the further development of psychology as a science because bundling the focus of various areas of psychology into one specific project not only pressures psychology to develop new theoretical tools and concepts in the process as well enhancing the already existing concepts, but also might potentially lead psychology to form a more coherent internal structure. By this is meant additional descriptions that document in detail the relationship between various branches of psychology within the framework of this science. Further, the completion of this project would be beneficial to psychology insofar as it would allow deeper access to the operations and inner workings of the human mind, hence bringing psychology significantly closer to its ultimate vision of becoming a science of the human psyche. In fact, what guarantees this tremendous benefit to psychology is that the design of a psychological theory of experience must be guided by the following question: What are the activities that take place in the mind when the mind introduces or presents an "experienced object" to the consciousness of an experiencing subject?

Accordingly, any potentially successful theory would have to spell out all the conditions, all the factors and all the activities involved, including how the mind monitors and processes these activities through which an appearance appears in its unique or particular way as a state of awareness.

Chapter 10
Applying Naturalism

REVISITING OLD TOPICS NATURALISTICALLY

In the discussion of Naturalism and the Discipline of Naturalistic Studies in the previous chapters, Naturalism was defined as a way of practicing philosophy using reflective, analytical and critical thinking methods within the frame work of science by adopting scientific methods of justification and procedures for seeking knowledge, including scientific findings and established facts. Further, it was stated that Naturalism has no particular agenda or purpose on its own; however, its method could be used for various constructive social, political and cultural objectives, such as debunking myths and cultural rituals that are harmful to human wellbeing, as well as exposing charlatans, demagogues or mass manipulators who aim at taking advantage of individuals or groups.

IGNORANCE

In the history of philosophy, "ignorance" has been primarily been defined through normative methods. In the context of naturalistic philosophy, the task of defining "ignorance" descriptively would fall under the domain of social sciences, including social psychology. A descriptive account would aim at explaining how "ignorance" is identified and how it is applied or used socially and culturally, including how it spreads within the community and the socio-economic factors that contribute to its growth (see the history of Nazi Germany, McCarthyism, Witch hunt, Islamic fundamentalism, Russian Nationalism, etc.). It is important to note that since a naturalistic account would not be metaphysical, it does not aim at defining what ignorance IS.

A NATURALISTIC INTRODUCTION TO PHILOSOPHY

ASSIGNMENT 1:

Would you consider these as symptoms of ignorance?

"I am / we are chosen people, special, member of an elite group."
"I already know the truth."
Overconfident about one's own opinions (lack of humility)
Making hasty judgments (superficial perspective)
Too quick to give recommendations (without being asked)

ASSIGNMENT 2:

Do you agree with the following definition of ignorance? Explain why or why not.

Definition: Tendency to PREJUDGE things and jump to conclusions without sufficient knowledge, information or evidence. Examples: Sexism and Racism.

ASSIGNMENT 3:

Is Euro-centrism in academia motivated by ignorance?

ASSIGNMENT 4:

Does ignorance assume that everything is a matter of opinion? For example, since everyone is entitled to his or her own opinion, facts / factual claims would also be opinions.

ASSIGNMENT 5:

Do cultures promote ignorance?

Examples:

Demanding obedience (be a team player)

Producing myths in the name of making factual claims about the world (how the world came into existence and how it functions)

Promoting exclusivity (we are better than them)

Making unfounded claims about other cultures / people (how members of other cultures think, live and act).

ASSIGNMENT 6:

Do religions celebrate ignorance by demanding blind faith and trust?
Examples:
Generalizing and categorizing people (certain people are inherently good or bad)
Promoting exclusivity ("only **we** will be saved")

ASSIGNMENT 7:

Does the Texas GOP Promote Ignorance based on the statement below (Texas GOP rejects 'critical thinking' skills. By Valerie Strauss July 9, 2012 Washington Post):

Knowledge-Based Education – We oppose the teaching of Higher Order Thinking Skills (HOTS) (values clarification), critical thinking skills and similar programs that are simply a relabeling of Outcome-Based Education (OBE) (mastery learning) which focus on behavior modification and have the purpose of challenging the student's fixed beliefs and undermining parental authority.

A NATURALISTIC INTRODUCTION TO PHILOSOPHY

THOUGHT EXPERIMENT

Consistent with the use of a priori assumptions in a naturalistic framework (see chapters 6 and 7), we can presuppose that "valuing self-worth" is an important, if not the most motivating factor that could jumpstart naturalistic interpretations about how ignorance is generated socially and culturally, how it spreads within the community and which socio-economic factors contribute to its growth.

Such a priori commitments are not unusual in the history of philosophy; Nietzsche presupposed *"the will to Power"* as something that all humans value intrinsically, while Utilitarians presupposed "seeking pleasure," or happiness as the only thing intrinsically valued.

The difference between these proposals and the proposed a priori assumption "valuing self-worth" is that while "the will to Power" or "the desire to seek happiness" are unchanging and therefore inflexible metaphysical assumptions about human nature, "valuing self-worth" is a temporary instrumental assumption used to make a naturalistic account possible.

The following account is an example or model for demonstrating how a descriptive and empirical approach could address issues related to ignorance without making any factual claim about human nature.

The thought experiment begins with the assumption <u>that humans have a tendency (psychological need) to feel important or valuable, and that "ignorant ideas or beliefs" are the most accessible tools (available to many individuals) for satisfying this psychological need for self-worth.</u> For example, individuals may take pride in the type of lifestyle they have, what social community, club or culture they belong to, or which God they worship. Accordingly, individuals enjoy their privileged status, or self-worth, by believing in what they do and believe. A naturalistic account would have **to** include descriptions about how individuals strategize differently depending on their situations and their available options, and perhaps engage in deceptions to affirm their self-worth.

Self-affirmation could express itself in the following form: *I am/we are entitled to a position of power, special treatments, etc.* The most visible place for this type of self-affirmations is the back of people's cars, known as bumper stickers; they let us know what the driver of that car is proud of / how he or she defines self-worth. Finding self-worth could also manifest itself through having a collection of cars, motorcycles, stamps, rare kind of cats or dogs, or artifacts. The bottom line is that the reason can be anything, and if individuals cannot find a reason, then they will create one, as long as it makes the person feel "privileged".

These explanations should sound familiar to any student of philosophy (see Nietzschian perspectivism and its pragmatist account of truth): "Truth is the kind of error without which a certain species of life could not live. The value for life is ultimately decisive". Including Nietzsche in the proposed model here, individuals will choose the interpretation that is most believable to everyone, including themselves, for feeling special (priding in a political party or cheering for an athletic team). Other examples include living in a certain part of town, having a degree from a particular high school or university, or being a member of an exclusive society, club or association. In short, all of these beliefs or interpretations are valued instrumentally only in so far that they make one feel special or important.

POTENTIAL NATURALISTIC ACCOUNT

A naturalistic account would have to explore any causal link that may exist between intellectual abilities of individuals and the types of beliefs they will accept that promote self-worth. Such an account may include scientific predictions about the vulnerability of individuals to certain types of demagogueries. Generally speaking, it is possible that any form of demagoguery that oversimplifies views has a greater chance of being accepted as true belief. This possibility raises the question of whether or not "convenience" is a factor for accepting an idea as true, since some individuals prefer beliefs that are pre-established and dictated from an authority (person or institution, culture) over the painful process of thinking independently and critically. Additionally, ideas that are intellectually accessible to everyone are presented in a "black and white" fashion and their simplicity makes them more popular. The convenience factor of certain simplistic ideas can promote some forms of extremism, such as some people are inherently bad, or that "bad people" are supposedly identifiable ("Jews", "women with red hair", individuals with certain skin color, etc.). Consistent with problem solving research in psychology (discussed in chapter 8), superficial ideas are used as a solution to a problem (i.e. "how can I feel important or superior?"). The false analogy committed in this context, "I am different than them/ I don't look like them and therefore I must be better," is adopted only to serve self-glorification.

All things considered, oversimplified ideas do not require critical reflection, and they tend to be consumed by people who lack intellectual abilities. Accordingly, one may call the use of ideas solely for self-promotion or self-esteem "ignorance". It should be noted that the approach used in this example is not metaphysical because no idea IS "ignorant" per se, but rather that the instrumental use of simplistic ideas by ignoring existing facts (committing suppressed evidence and / or begging the question fallacies) to achieve a self-serving objective such as feeling good or feeling superior makes these ideas ignorant (for example, creationism).

Finally, this proposal, while it is naturalistic, it is not scientific since it was NOT developed using scientific methods. Naturalism only demands CONSISTENCY with science to be critical and analytic about various issues without competing with science in making factual claims.

It is worth noting that consistency with science in a naturalistic framework is achieved using already existing scientific theories to develop explanations / interpretations, although stretching or extending scientific explanations beyond the boundaries in which they were originally developed is not permissible for making factual claims; however, the consistency with science as it was discussed in chapter 6 provides the most dependable and promising framework for practicing philosophy analytically, reflectively and critically.

RACISM AND POLITICAL CORRECTNESS

Racism has been a serious social political and ethical issue for a long time and not just in the United States, but also worldwide. Unfortunately, racism is still an ongoing problem in spite of major socio-cultural improvement or "progress". What is particularly wrong about racism is that it makes us blind. It prevents us from making and learning from experiences. Further, racism is morally wrong because it prevents us from seeing an individual; instead, we see a member or representative of a group. In essence, when racism is present, the humanity and dignity of a person is reduced to being a member of a group, be it social, ethnic, etc.

Since racism confines experience and any knowledge that is then formed, it often leads to misrepresentations, rather than allowing for less biased experience, and hence, more objective feedback. There are many possible explanations for how racism has managed to survive over centuries. A potential cause of racism's extended lifespan is denial. Members of society often recognize racism as a problem that exists, but as something that is always there but never here; no one believes they have seen racism practiced in person. Because racism has become an invisible issue, very few recognize it even though it permeates their lives. Every so often we are given an unpleasant reminder of existing racial tension, like the recent riots that have occurred in Baltimore, Ferguson and Los Angeles, which tell us that racism lurks beneath the surface.

The problem with modern racism is that it is harder to detect and consequently, we prematurely conclude (perhaps accompanied with wishful thinking) that racism belongs to the past and no longer exist in our community. One might even use the Civil Rights movement and political correctness that is rampant in today's society as claims that racism is dead.

In fact, due to the difficulty in identifying racism as present in our daily life, it may well be that a new definition is needed. Today's racism appears differently than it did half a century ago. The old understanding of racism relied on demeaning comments, insults and violence, but the current appearance of racism is far more complex and hidden, making it harder to detect due to its passive and indirect appearances. There are many signs pointing towards a state of denial in today's society. On one hand we would like to pretend that we live in a color blind society, while on the other hand, we are reminded on a daily basis that we are not yet there.

Many people witness racially charged aggressions but fail to realize the full extent of their meaning. It can appear as treating a person's college degree as inferior or the result of affirmative action, undervaluing a person's professional judgment, or considering certain accents or dialects to sound uneducated and uncultivated. Today's racism appears in a less obvious form by treating minorities' credentials or characteristics like disvalued currency, by not taking them seriously. An example would be when an idea is not judged based on its merit, but rather it is prejudged based on an assumed link between someone's ethnic or cultural upbringing, and the statement asserted. In such cases a fallacy is committed known as "argument against the person circumstantial." Even without knowing this fallacy, one might instinctively consider this treatment rude and disrespectful. This attitude is comparable to the attitude towards women of major Western philosophers like Plato, Kant and Nietzsche, who believed women are guided by their instinctive maternal nature of nurture and care, and hence disqualified and excluded from philosophical discourses. A more current example is the belief that certain races lack intellectual ability and should be excluded from professional fields and discourses for which they may very well be qualified. These same individuals will often be second guessed and find their work doubted.

What makes the modern brand of racism especially dangerous is the person may not be aware of their own prejudice. Harvard University Professor Chester M. Pierce identified these subtle insults or invalidations as "microaggressions." A microaggression is any statement or attitude that conveys a generalization and implies that a person's race or culture is inferior. These hidden meanings can even be accidental or intended as compliments. For example, statements like, "Of course you did well, you're Asian," or, "Wow, you got into that university? You're lucky that there's Affirmative Action," may seem innocent to the person stating them. However, the person for whom these compliments were intended might pick up on the indirect implications of these sentences; they devalue the work of an individual and attribute it to their race.

Generally speaking, today's racism is often indirect or invisible, but there are some indicators that could give away a racist's tendencies. Second guessing everyone in a certain race or culture's thoughts and opinions, and making them the subject of a tougher scrutiny which would naturally lead to actually finding flaws or weaknesses, are both possible indicators.

All things considered, the main problem regarding race relations in America is relying too much on clichés. We have to free ourselves from our stereotypes, even the cliché of racists being only white, old, and southern! The fact of the matter is that anyone can be racist, white people, African American, Hispanic, Native American, Asian people, individuals with middle eastern background, native Alaskan, Russian etc. In addition, racism can occur anywhere, in elementary schools, on college campuses, at a corporate board meeting, in church, etc. To internalize the notion that racism is not limited to any particular relationships or occasions, we have to free ourselves from clichés or stereotypes. Accordingly, as we do not judge the validity of a philosophical proposal based on how "philosophical" the person looks or appears, we should not use naïve and superficial cultural views to determine what a racist looks like. The notion that stereotypes or clichés prevent a genuine change in our hearts and in our minds must be taken seriously, because only then will we be able to cure this social and cultural disease of racism.

In summary, it can be stated that racism still exists and interferes with daily life in America, because we are unable to see it or identify it due to its ability to adapt by finding new forms of expression. Further, stereotypes or cultural clichés about which groups or individuals are racist prevent our ability to see when racism occurs, and it is precisely in this context that a naturalistic approach could demystify our cultural views about race relations. A naturalistic analysis of racism would be critical and reflective, and consistent with well-practiced science, accompanied by flexibility of perspectives that will be able to identify the hidden practices of racism. In other words, a naturalistic account could help to expose and remove cultural blindness towards racism, and shed light on its existence, making it visible when it occurs.

In addition to the complexity of today's racism, political correctness and socio-political reactions to the issue of racism have become obstacles by complicating the issue instead of reducing cultural misconceptions. Political correctness eases the pain of the troubled history of the United States and creates the illusion of equal treatment in our society, which makes racism even more stealth or difficult to see racism when it occurs. Above all, political correctness prevents a genuine long-term solution by prohibiting a straight forward, honest dialogue concerning race relations.

Imagine an alcoholic who is in therapy, but insists on not using the word "alcohol" during the sessions. Obviously, it would be absurd to think that he would have any realistic chance of addressing the real addiction problem without acknowledging to what he is addicted. Similarly, any constructive social dialogue about racism would require honest and direct conversations about the prejudicial views that political correctness forbids us from discussing. Such discussion would have to explore why or in which context African Americans, for example, consider "white people" as racially biased as often as Caucasians have a tendency to view African Americans in a certain way. The bottom line is that we must face this problem head on instead of looking for scapegoats or pointing fingers at guilty parties from the past.

A genuine social dialogue requires a soul searching of our common cultural views, with the goal to seek clarity as well as to demystify cultural nonsense instead of adding popular or more acceptable phrases. There is a lack of social dialogue about race relations in America due to political correctness which prevents us from focusing on genuine racial issues, and prohibits meaningful constructive conversations. In fact, the overuse of political correctness has led to an unintended but hidden social policy of "fake it till you make it."

Political correctness is not a permanent solution to the racial problem in America, since it functions only as a "painkiller" with side effects, keeping us in a state of denial, creating the illusion that racial problems are solved. Political correctness is often used in shock or disgust that someone would dare suggest the presence of racism in their environment. It also infers the immediate disqualification of any unconventional stance on the causes, or solutions, of racial prejudice. The "inappropriateness" of certain language or actions is an indication that certain expressions and actions are undesirable.

There is no doubt that political correctness contributed to cultural changes and improvements in American society, but the problem that it has created on the side has become an obstacle in finding a solution for race issues because it demands "approved" vocabulary and language at a time when we need honest and straightforward dialogue. Specifically, political correctness intimidates people from talking freely since individuals are constantly worried about how their ideas might be perceived, or that what they intend to say might come out "the wrong way" and make them sound racist. The semi fascist cultural climate created by political correctness forces individuals to practice self-censorship by not saying anything at all just to be safe. For example, affirmative action requires educators to make students feel comfortable before they will share their true ideas in the class. Often, students hesitate before sharing ideas and opinions due to the poisoned cultural climate caused by political correctness.

All in all, additional studies are needed, including the exploration of socio-cultural thoughts through interviews and empirical studies, in order to identify the psychological issues in racism.

Another way to demonstrate the unintended problem arising from political correctness can be referred to as the "weaponization" of political correctness. Weaponization occurs when unqualified individuals use race issues as weapons to manipulate their employers until they are promoted to a higher position or hired as a full-time employee. Yet again, we find that issues such as the one just stated do not fit the popular narrative of prejudice, and are unlikely to be seen as legitimate racism in the modern climate.

All things considered, while political correctness has been helpful in the past, its unintended side effects are now greater than its benefits. The only way to combat the infection of racism in America is through the ability to differentiate between prejudiced thinking that permeates day to day life, and the exploration of the demons that haunt our country today. For sure, this isn't a problem that will disappear by turning a blind eye on existing social and cultural facts. In contrary, we need to collect more facts to overcome racism in the future; based on the potential solutions and explanations offered in previous chapters, the context of naturalism provides the most reliable / dependable framework for doing so.

Made in the USA
Middletown, DE
02 August 2016